Information Tools for Industry

Second Edition

Produced by the
Southern Technology Council
A division of the Southern Growth Policies Board

In collaboration with
The Precision Metalforming Association
National Tooling and Machining Association

And with industrial extension agencies and service providers in Alabama, Georgia, Kentucky, North Carolina, South Carolina, Tennessee, Virginia, and West Virginia

By

Scott J. Doron, Southern Growth Policies Board

Nancy E. McCrea, National Association of State Development Agencies
(formerly with the Southern Growth Policies Board)

Ben S. Vickery, Southern Technology Council

Louis G. Tornatzky, Southern Technology Council

This catalog was produced under a contract from the
Appalachian Regional Commission
Contract No. 94-28   CO-11482-94-I-302-0204

May 1996

This catalog was produced under a contract from the
Appalachian Regional Commission
Contract No. 94-28
CO-11482-94-I-302-0204

ISBN 0-927-364-05-0

Information Tools for Industry, Second Edition is available in electronic
form on the World Wide Web at the Southern Technology Council and
Southern Growth Policies Board home page, *http://www.southern.org*.

A traditional print version is available free-of-charge (while supplies last)
for any manufacturing company or service provider organization
located in the Appalachian region of the STC states.

For others, single copies of the report may be ordered for $25 each,
including postage and handling.

To order, or for additional information, please address:

Southern Technology Council
P.O. Box 12293
Research Triangle Park, NC 27709
VOICE   (919) 941-5145
FAX   (919) 941-5594
E-MAIL   stc@southern.org

TABLE OF CONTENTS

Within each Problem Area Focus section,
the tools are arranged in alphabetical order.

CHAPTER 3 — MARKET AND BUSINESS DEVELOPMENT

CHAPTER 4 – ORGANIZATIONAL REENGINEERING AND REDESIGN

INTRODUCTION

The Southern Technology Council (STC) developed this catalog of "Information Tools for Industry" to help smaller manufacturers that are struggling to keep up with rapid changes in their business environment. Specifically, this catalog is based on the belief that, more than ever, companies are in need of useful and easy-to-use sources of information. The purpose of the catalog is to describe briefly a wide range of information tools that companies may find useful.

This is the second edition of the "Information Tools for Industry" catalog and as such represents an expansion and improvement on the earlier version. The number of tool entries have been increased about 75 percent, although the addition of some catalogs-as-tools makes a precise count of individual tools very difficult. Of particular note, this edition has several new entries in the areas of coatings and plastics processing. Some entries from the first edition were eliminated as tools were withdrawn from the market or organizations ceased operations.

The tools included in this catalog range from books and videotapes on management issues to software systems designed to help companies with complex business decisions, to assessment methods for everything from training needs to waste reduction. In selecting tools, STC tried to identify products that were "transportable," that could be easily used by companies, and that could add value to their business decisions. A survey conducted by STC at the outset of this project identified six categories of information needs for metalworking companies, and the catalog is organized around these categories: 1) Technology; 2) Human Resources; 3) Financing and Business Practices; 4) Regulatory; 5) Organizational Reengineering and Design; and 6) Market and Business Development.

The project is supported by the Appalachian Regional Commission (ARC). Partners in the project include the National Tooling and Machining Association (NTMA), the Precision Metalforming Association (PMA), the Georgia Institute of Technology, the Industrial Technology Institute (ITI), and the manufacturing extension programs in the states of Alabama, Georgia, Kentucky, North Carolina, South Carolina, Tennessee, Virginia, and West Virginia. For this second edition of the catalog we have also been indebted to the Society of the Plastics Industry and the National Paint and Coatings Association for their cooperation. The American Society for Training and Development (ASTD) continues to be a major participant. All were helpful in identifying and providing tools for the catalog. Other tools were identified through industry and technical journals, federal programs, and the companies themselves. This is by no means an exhaustive collection of industry tools. STC plans to continually update and amend the tool catalog to include newly identified products. We welcome suggestions of additional entries or tool providers.

We would like to thank all the tool providers who submitted their products for inclusion in the catalog. STC has attempted to collect as much information as possible about the tools listed; however, the inclusion of specific products is not be construed as an endorsement by STC or the Appalachian Regional Commission. If you have questions about any of the tools listed, feel free to contact STC or the vendor directly.

The STC team that summarized the tools for this edition included Scott Doron and Ben Vickery; Nancy McCrea contributed summaries for the first edition that are also included in this version. Kristina Ahlén, Yolanda Batts, and Lou Tornatzky edited individual summaries, while Robert Donnan and Leah Totten edited the overall manuscript for this second edition. Ms. Totten also created the catalog's design and managed its production and printing; she previously contributed an overall edit, design, and production for the first edition. Annette Roper offered a range of administrative services.

CHAPTER 1

FINANCING AND BUSINESS PRACTICES

BUSINESS MANAGEMENT AIDS

DESCRIPTION

Business Management Aids is an "MBA in a notebook"—a 300-page collection of business reports. It is a storehouse of materials about business issues facing metalworking firms. Topic areas include accounting, labor relations, Occupational Safety and Health Administration (OSHA) and Environmental Protection Agency (EPA) compliance, taxes, insurance, and training. Each report is short and concise, and delivers pragmatic information on managing a shop's people and finances. The National Tooling and Machining Association (NTMA) updates the report as necessary.

HOW DO I USE IT?

The notebook is arranged according to topic area. Users interested in a particular area can look up those sections in the manual.

COST

One copy of the handbook is free to NTMA members. Members receive revisions and updates as they are published. Additional copies of the report cost $49.95. This tool is available only to NTMA members.

STRENGTHS AND WEAKNESSES FOR USERS

The notebook offers a comprehensive source of business information specifically for metalworking firms. Although the report is applicable to all sizes of metalworking firms, it is of particular assistance in bringing professional business acumen to smaller metalworking shops. This notebook is available only to NTMA member companies.

USER BASE

NTMA consists of more than 3,000 tooling and machining companies in 56 chapters throughout the U.S. Sixty-five percent of the members have 20 employees or less.

USER SUPPORT

	N/A	Available	Comments
Consultants	x		
Documentation	x		
Training Classes	x		
Telephone Support		x	

VENDOR CONTACT

The National Tooling & Machining Association
9300 Livingston Road
Ft. Washington, MD 20744
VOICE   (301) 248-6200
FAX   (301) 248-7104

BuySmart! ®

DESCRIPTION

BuySmart! is a personal computer-based expert system for evaluating and selecting applications software for manufacturers and distributors. The *BuySmart!* methodology guides the selection of the appropriate software for business needs. The *BuySmart!* database of more than 1,700 requirements helps differentiate systems for job shop, repetitive process, and for food, pharmaceutical, and defense industries. It comes with a directory of applications software for manufacturers and distributors. *ChooseSmart!*, a workshop, provides instruction on the selection and acquisition process.

HOW DO I USE IT?

The *BuySmart!* methodology guides users through the Request for Proposal (RFP) process. As users describe their businesses, *BuySmart!* identifies detailed system requirements and software features that are important to each functional area of the company. *BuySmart!* allows users to select from a complete list of functional requirements and lets users define their unique needs. The *BuySmart!* Applications Software Directory lets users peruse hundreds of software vendors and packages by platforms, modules/functions, databases, LANs, CASE tools, and more.

COST

BuySmart! costs $4,500. *ChooseSmart!* costs $9,000.

STRENGTHS AND WEAKNESSES FOR USERS

BuySmart! avoids problems associated with software implementation by ensuring a complete definition of functional needs and involving management in the specification process. *BuySmart!* allows the user to get consensus among widely differing functional groups for new software systems. The program produces a detailed listing of system specifications—but not software products—for the manufacturer. The *ChooseSmart!* workshops provide instruction on the selection and acquisition process, facilitation of the RFP preparation, and delivery of a short list of the software packages that best match client requirements.

USER BASE

BuySmart! has been used by several of the Manufacturing Technology Centers in business system software definition, evaluation, and selection for small and mid-sized manufacturing companies in both product-driven and job shop settings. It is also used by consultants to perform cost studies.

USER SUPPORT

	N/A	Available	Comments
Consultants	x		*ChooseSmart!* is a fixed-fee consulting service to assist companies with software selection, including the development of a fully qualified vendor short-list.
Documentation	x		

	N/A	Available	Comments
Training Classes		x	Training classes are part of *ChooseSmart!*.
Telephone Support	x		

VENDOR CONTACT

Expert Buying Systems
P.O. Box 4739
Vancouver, WA 98662-0739
Attn: Bill Capron
VOICE (360) 260-1896 or (800) 832-6434
FAX (360) 263-5235

CAPITOL CAPITAL: GOVERNMENT RESOURCES FOR HIGH-TECHNOLOGY COMPANIES

DESCRIPTION

Capitol Capital is a 214-page book that describes federal and state government resources for high-technology companies. These resources include funds for R&D (Chapter 1), tapping into federal laboratories (Chapter 2), defense conversion and dual-use programs (Chapter 3), manufacturing programs (Chapter 4), sources of domestic financing (Chapter 5), and international financing (Chapter 6). The book also has a chapter of seven case studies that describes success stories of accessing programs and services.

HOW DO I USE IT?

The book is well-organized, defines key terms, lists numerous points of contact (including names, phone numbers, and addresses), and is well-indexed. A 23-page appendix is devoted entirely to points of contact. It is full of hard-to-find and useful information.

COST

The book costs $29.95 for members of the American Electronics Association (AEA) and $49.95 for non-members. Add $5 for shipping and handling per publication.

STRENGTHS AND WEAKNESSES FOR USERS

The book's strengths lie in its comprehensiveness and level of detail in terms of contact information. A potential weakness is that contact information changes, and information in the book becomes rapidly outdated. However, the current edition was published in 1994 and should be useful for some time.

USER BASE

According to AEA, more than 3000 copies are in distribution.

USER SUPPORT

	N/A	Available	Comments
Consultants		x	
Documentation		x	
Training Classes		x	
Telephone Support	x		

VENDOR CONTACT

American Electronics Association Customer Service Center
5201 Great America Parkway
P.O. Box 54990
Santa Clara, CA 95056-0990
VOICE   (800) 284-4232
FAX   (408) 970-8565

THE COATINGS AGENDA AMERICA 1995/96

DESCRIPTION

The first edition of *The Coatings Agenda America 1995/96* is an annual overview of the North American paint and coatings industry. The publication is a sister book to *The Coatings Agenda*, a three-year-old report established as the leading publication addressing the European paint and coatings industry.

HOW DO I USE IT?

The book consists of articles about industry challenges and achievements written by senior people in the paint and coatings industry. The book divides into three sections: management, markets, and technology.

COST

Contact vendor.

STRENGTHS AND WEAKNESSES FOR USERS

The management section consists of insights into the industry by directors of major paint companies and representatives from paint associations. In the markets section, the geographical element of the coatings industry is discussed, and major suppliers evaluate issues in such areas as decorative, protective, automotive and industrial coatings. The technology section features summaries of the latest developments by suppliers of raw materials, equipment, and supply-side services. The report ends with a directory listing of selected product and service providers.

USER BASE

The National Painting and Coating Association (NPCA) is a voluntary, nonprofit trade association representing approximately 500 paint and coatings manufacturers, raw materials suppliers and distributors. Collectively, NPCA's membership produces approximately 75 percent of the total dollar-volume of paints and industrial coatings sold in the United States.

USER SUPPORT

	N/A	Available	Comments
Consultants	x		
Documentation	x		
Training Classes	x		
Telephone Support	x		

VENDOR CONTACT

Campden Publishing
Threeways House
40-44 Clipstone Street
London W1P 8LX
United Kingdom
VOICE   +44 (0) 171 636 1600

FINANCIAL AND OPERATING RATIOS SURVEY

DESCRIPTION

This report is an annual survey of plastics society member companies. The survey presents financial and operating ratios in areas such as assets and liabilities, net sales, pretax and after-tax income, cost of sales, overhead, depreciation, inventory, and administrative expenses. Figures are sub-divided by facility sales, processing method, profitability, and geographic location.

HOW DO I USE IT?

Employees in plastics processing companies can compare their ratios to ratios of similar facilities with similar characteristics. Such analysis should help management make strategic decisions about use of resources.

COST

Members of The Society of the Plastics Industry, $100; non-members, $200.

STRENGTHS AND WEAKNESSES FOR USERS

Since the data is compiled from society members, it gives real yardsticks for facility comparisons. Annual publication means current data.

USER BASE

Not Available.

USER SUPPORT

	N/A	Available	Comments
Consultants	x		
Documentation		x	
Training Classes	x		
Telephone Support	x		

VENDOR CONTACT

The Society of the Plastics Industry, Inc.
1275 K Street, NW, #400
Washington, DC 20005-4006
VOICE (202) 371-5293

LEARNERFIRST: BENCHMARKING 1.0 FOR WINDOWS

DESCRIPTION

Benchmarking is a quality improvement method that measures the performance of employees, products, equipment, and processes, and sets goals for improvement. The *LearnerFirst* software takes the complex benchmarking process and breaks it into simple, step-by-step activities. The process begins with identifying benchmark subjects and then proceeds into developing measures, implementing changes, and measuring the impact of the changes.

HOW DO I USE IT?

The software breaks the benchmarking process into 19 easy-to-follow lessons that are organized like chapters in a book. Users begin by analyzing their businesses and identifying the appropriate factors to benchmark: a product, a manufacturing process, a business process, or an equipment item. The software then guides users through the benchmarking process. Users collect internal information, do original research and interviews, visit company facilities, and study competitors to determine their strengths. *Benchmarking 1.0* then helps organize information into a database and creates reports of the results. Finally, users identify corrective actions, develop a plan, get management approval, make the changes, and track the impact of their changes.

All company information is stored in the application's custom database. Each item that is benchmarked can be saved as an individual file. At the end of every activity, users can print reports or paste reports into word processing documents so reports can be formatted according to user's needs. *LearnerFirst: Benchmarking 1.0* can be used with an IBM personal computer or compatible with at least a 20 MHz 386 processor.

COST

The cost is $425. Prices do not include shipping and processing.

STRENGTHS AND WEAKNESSES FOR USERS

Using questions that provoke active and thoughtful responses from users, the benchmarking program leads users to create their own ideas, insights, and solutions. The programs are fast, highly interactive, and easy to use. Benchmarking requires that users obtain management support and form a benchmarking committee. These steps require a commitment of time and resources, but the system helps prepare the information for managing these steps.

USER BASE

LearnerFirst: Benchmarking 1.0 is designed for larger business environments. Some of the companies that have used the software are Fortune 500 companies, but the system is appropriate for companies of all sizes and all levels of expertise.

USER SUPPORT

	N/A	Available	Comments
Consultants	x		
Documentation		x	Includes *Learner's Guide* and on-line help system.
Training Classes		x	
Telephone Support		x	*LearnerFirst* offers technical support by phone, fax, and email. Both services are available for 90 days for users who complete and return their registration card.

VENDOR CONTACT

LearnerFirst, Inc.
1075 13th Street South
Birmingham, Alabama 35205
VOICE   (205) 934-9182
FAX   (205) 934-1037
E-MAIL   LearnFast@aol.com

THE NTIS CATALOG OF PRODUCTS AND SERVICES, 1995-1996

DESCRIPTION

The *National Technical Information Service (NTIS) Catalog* contains more than 2.5 million titles and covers more than 375 scientific, technical, engineering and business-related subjects. Products include audiocassettes and videotapes, technical reports, periodicals, databases, computer software, diskettes, CD-ROMs, and on-line services.

How Do I Use It?

The catalog is arranged according to subject area. Users interested in a particular area would look up the appropriate sections of the catalog. The catalog also contains a list of other NTIS product information, including the free *Fedworld Preview Database*.

Cost

The catalog is free.

Strengths and Weaknesses for Users

This free publication is a valuable tool to stay current in critical areas. It offers a wealth of new products and services that can help expand a company's business opportunities.

User Base

NTIS user base includes industry, contractors, state and local regulators, and researchers.

User Support

	N/A	Available	Comments
Consultants		x	
Documentation		x	
Training Classes		x	
Telephone Support	x		

Vendor Contact

The National Technical Information Service
5285 Port Royal Rd.
Springfield, VA 22161
VOICE   (703) 487-4650
FAX   (703) 321-8547
E-MAIL   orders@ntis.fedworld.gov

Quote order number NTIS PR-827.

Operating Costs and Executive Compensation Report

Description

Managers need to know how their company's operating costs compare to other firms in the same industry. This report from the National Tooling and Machining Association (NTMA) details this information based on a nationwide survey of NTMA members. The annual report compares financial performance between companies in the same sales, and product or service categories. Managers can use the reports to justify compensation if challenged by the Internal Revenue Service.

How Do I Use It?

The report includes national cost averages with comparisons between similar types of firms. The report is useful as a benchmark when dealing with bankers or the Internal Revenue Service.

Cost

The survey is free for NTMA members participating in the survey. NTMA members who do not return the survey questionnaire may purchase the report for $500. This tool is only available to members of NTMA.

Strengths and Weaknesses for Users

No other source provides such detailed information specifically for the metalworking industry. Cost may be prohibitive for non-survey participants.

User Base

NTMA consists of more than 3,000 tooling and machining companies in 56 chapters throughout the U.S. Sixty-five percent of the members have 20 employees or less.

User Support

	N/A	Available	Comments
Consultants		x	
Documentation		x	
Training Classes		x	
Telephone Support	x		

Vendor Contact

The National Tooling & Machining Association
9300 Livingston Road
Ft. Washington, MD 20744
VOICE (301) 248-6200
FAX (301) 248-7104

WINNING GOVERNMENT GRANTS AND CONTRACTS FOR YOUR SMALL BUSINESS

Description

Winning Government Grants and Contracts for Your Small Business features proven strategies for finding, applying for, and winning contracts. The book focuses on the billions of government dollars earmarked for small business owners, in such diverse areas as research, job training, product development, consulting, and testing. The book, written by Mark Rowh, offers an overview of government programs that issue grants and awards.

How Do I Use It?

Winning Government Grants and Contracts for Your Small Business covers programs that range from the highly technical to providing job training for the unemployed to grants and contracts available to minority-owned firms. The 190-page book explains how to locate many potential funding sources and includes a glossary of terms and acronyms, as well as a sample grant proposal.

Cost

Winning Government Grants and Contracts for Your Small Business is available to National Council for Urban Economic Development (CUED) members for $29.95 and to non-members for $33.95.

Strengths and Weaknesses for Users

Written in an informative yet easy-to-read format, *Winning Government Grants and Contracts for Your Small Business* provides solid advice and helpful guidelines on how small firms can compete for government grants and awards.

User Base

The book is available through the National Council for Urban Economic Development, a leading national organization serving economic development practitioners. CUED was founded in 1967 and currently has over 1,500 members.

User Support

	N/A	Available	Comments
Consultants	x		
Documentation	x		
Training Classes	x		
Telephone Support	x		

Vendor Contact

National Council for Urban Economic Development
1730 K Street
Washington, DC 20006
VOICE   (202) 223-4735
FAX   (202) 223-4745

CHAPTER 2

HUMAN RESOURCES

ANALYSIS FOR IMPROVING PERFORMANCE: TOOLS FOR DIAGNOSING ORGANIZATIONS & DOCUMENTING WORKPLACE EXPERTISE

DESCRIPTION

This 286-page book includes 17 pages of master diagnosis and documentation forms and more than 50 exhibits or examples of the forms being applied. It is designed to give the human resources manager or corporate executive a set of tools and methods for analyzing key company functions or operations. This is often considered a critical preparatory step to efforts such as TQM, business practice reengineering, and training and development. The approach involves two phases: performance diagnosis and documentation of expertise, and three levels of information-gathering and analysis. Analysis results include clear documentation of the existing work system and its problems and plans for improvement.

HOW DO I USE IT?

The book lies somewhere between a "cookbook" and a conceptual treatment of performance improvement issues. The user needs to read through the book once and then go back and concentrate on those chapters most relevant to the situation at hand. The examples, practical advice, and checklists are quite useful but fall just short of being an unambiguous road map.

COST

Analysis for Improving Performance: Tools for Diagnosing Organizations & Documenting Workplace Expertise is available for $32.95 plus $3.50 shipping and handling.

STRENGTHS AND WEAKNESSES FOR USERS

The book provides an excellent mix of necessary conceptual background as well as specific tools and procedures. It will be a useful resource for a corporate manager undertaking a reengineering or improvement program. It is not the single resource necessary to do the job, although it does point the user toward other references and resources.

USER BASE

This is a relatively new publication, but 2,500 copies are already in users' hands.

USER SUPPORT

	N/A	Available	Comments
Consultants	x		
Documentation	x		
Training Classes	x		
Telephone Support	x		

VENDOR CONTACT

Berrett-Koehler Publishers
155 Montgomery Street
San Francisco, CA 94104-4109
VOICE   (415) 288-0260 or
            (800) 929-2929

ASTD TRAINER'S TOOLKIT: EVALUATING THE RESULTS OF TRAINING

DESCRIPTION

This toolkit presents the actual evaluation forms, checklists, guidelines, models, and formulas used by corporations such as Johnson Wax, Amoco, and AT&T to evaluate their training results.

HOW DO I USE IT?

Newcomers to the field can see practical examples of training evaluation methods. Seasoned practitioners get an overview of other professionals' evaluation techniques. Both can use these tools to see how training pays off in both employee behavior and dollars and cents.

COST

The cost to ASTD members is $39. The cost to non-members is $59.

STRENGTHS AND WEAKNESSES FOR USERS

Although these instruments describe actual, currently used methods, readers need to remember that these are state-of-the-practice methods, not necessarily best practices. Value judgments are left to the reader, who can take the most appropriate methods from each instrument and modify them to fit individual company needs.

The program does not specifically focus on metalworking firms, though it will be of use to them.

USER BASE

Not available.

USER SUPPORT

	N/A	Available	Comments
Consultants	x		
Documentation	x		
Training Classes	x		
Telephone Support	x		

VENDOR CONTACT
ASTD Publishing Service
Priority Code IDT
P.O. Box 4856, Hampden Station
Baltimore, MD 21211

ASTD TRAINER'S TOOLKIT: NEEDS ASSESSMENT INSTRUMENTS AND MORE NEEDS ASSESSMENT INSTRUMENTS

DESCRIPTION
These two toolkits contain the actual training needs assessment instruments of a variety of organizations, including:

- Chase Manhattan Bank;
- Mayo Foundation;
- Tennessee Valley Authority;
- Honeywell;
- Sony;
- Chevron; and
- General Electric.

These practical instruments are reproduced verbatim, giving practitioners a bird's-eye view of current methods. Introductory material or journal articles describe the needs assessment process and how each instrument was used by its organization.

HOW DO I USE IT?
Newcomers to the field can see in these toolkits practical examples of what needs assessment is and how assessment instruments are developed. Seasoned practitioners get an overview of other professionals' techniques and tools. Both groups can use these tools to modify, expand, or strengthen their own needs assessment methods.

COST
The cost to ASTD members is $39. The cost to non-members is $59.

STRENGTHS AND WEAKNESSES FOR USERS
Although the toolkits contain actual needs assessment instruments, readers need to remember these are state-of-the-practice instruments, not necessarily best practices. Value judgments are left to

the reader, who can take the most appropriate methods from each instrument and modify them to fit individual company needs. The program does not specifically focus on metalworking firms, though it will be of use to them.

USER BASE

Not available.

USER SUPPORT

	N/A	Available	Comments
Consultants	x		
Documentation	x		
Training Classes	x		
Telephone Support	x		

VENDOR CONTACT

ASTD Publishing Service
Priority Code IDT
P.O. Box 4856, Hampden Station
Baltimore, MD 21211

THE ASTD TRAINING SUPPORT SOFTWARE DIRECTORY

DESCRIPTION

The ASTD Training Support Software Directory makes researching and buying training software easy. The directory describes hundreds of programs, detailing hardware and software requirements, LAN capability, interfacing, prices and many other product criteria. Software categories include:

- Training development (50 programs);
- Human resource planning (19 programs);
- Performance management (48 programs);
- Instructional design and development (44 programs);
- Conference and meeting management (30 programs);
- Management development (22 programs);
- Career development (16 programs);
- Organization development (27 programs); and
- TQM (40 programs).

HOW DO I USE IT?

The ASTD Training Support Software Directory is clearly written and well organized. Information is arranged so readers can:

- Look for a particular vendor;
- Look for a particular program;
- Look for a program that can perform a particular function;
- Look for programs that run on specific hardware or operating systems; and
- Find help selecting software.

COST

The cost to ASTD members is $125. The cost to non-members is $155.

STRENGTHS AND WEAKNESSES FOR USERS

User-friendly and reliable, the *ASTD Training Support Software Directory* is the first specialized directory of training-related software in which vendors have not paid for inclusion in the directory and which has very detailed program descriptions. Although many varieties of training software are included in this directory, computer-based training software is not. However, the directory does list other guides that include such software.

The program does not specifically focus on metalworking firms, though it will be of use to them.

USER BASE

Not available.

USER SUPPORT

	N/A	Available	Comments
Consultants	x		
Documentation	x		
Training Classes	x		
Telephone Support	x		

VENDOR CONTACT

ASTD Publishing Service
Priority Code IDT
P.O. Box 4856, Hampden Station
Baltimore, MD 21211

CADD SKILL STANDARDS DOCUMENT
(COMPUTER AIDED DRAFTING AND DESIGN)

DESCRIPTION

Published in April 1994, this booklet includes a list of fundamental generic CADD skills and their related academic skills. It also contains recommendations for instructor qualifications, equipment, and hours of study.

HOW DO I USE IT?

The booklet may be used as criteria to build a CADD training program that meets industry standards or as a benchmark for one's existing program.

COST

The *CADD Skill Standards Document* is available for $22.50.

STRENGTHS AND WEAKNESSES FOR USERS

This document contains generic (i.e., non-software specific) CADD Skills pertinent to training programs in industry as well as schools. It contains recommendations that address several aspects of a training program beyond the technical skills. It is not designed to be used as curriculum. The skills listed are fundamental to all disciplines and do not include high-end CADD skills like finite element analysis. This document will be updated annually.

USER BASE

This document was developed under a Department of Education matching grant given to the research arm of NACFAM (National Coalition for Advanced Manufacturing). Staff is now developing an assessment exam to assess a user's proficiency in CADD. NACFAM is a nonprofit 501(c)(3) membership organization working to create an infrastructure of policies and programs designed to raise all tiers of U.S. industry to world-class levels of productivity, quality and competitiveness.

USER SUPPORT

	N/A	Available	Comments
Consultants		x	
Documentation		x	Measurability supplement.
Training Classes		x	Referrals available.
Telephone Support		x	

VENDOR CONTACT

Ann Brennan
NACFAM—CADD Project
1331 Pennsylvania Ave., NW, Suite 1410 North
Washington, DC 20004
VOICE   (202) 662-8912
FAX   (202) 662-8964

CAREERTRACK SEMINARS AND TAPE TRAINING CATALOG

DESCRIPTION

CareerTrack helps people work smarter by developing training programs that help people gain new skills, build their power with other people, help them understand a changing world, and, above all, show them how to believe in themselves and find the courage to act on their dreams. CareerTrack trains people through five different training formats: Public Seminars, On-Site Seminars, Video Tape Programs, Audio Tape Programs and Customized Programs.

HOW DO I USE IT?

The catalog lists all the public seminars scheduled for the next four months, including the description, price, date, and city. It also lists all of the video and audio training tapes available with the price and length of tape. If there is something not imediately evident, just call the 800-number in the catalog to see if they have it.

COST

The catalog is free.

- The public seminars listed in the catalog are priced from $79 to 145.
- The videos cost $79.95 for a one-volume set, $299.95 for a four volume set.
- Audio tape programs cost $39.95 to $99.95.
- The price of the On-Site Seminars depends on factors such as the number of days the seminar lasts, the professional trainer chosen, and expenses.

STRENGTHS AND WEAKNESSES FOR USERS

CareerTrack offers one-stop shopping for all of one's training needs. There are over 120 video and audio training programs, and over 7,000 public seminars, offered each year.

USER BASE

Customers consist of individuals as well as the leading organizations in virtually every industry. They include 476 of the Fortune 500 companies—from Coca-Cola to AT&T to Boeing—and hundreds of local, state and federal government agencies. In addition, training has been provided for thousands of health care facilities, educational institutions, and small to mid-sized businesses.

USER SUPPORT

	N/A	Available	Comments
Consultants		x	
Documentation	x		
Training Classes		x	
Telephone Support		x	Personalized service for consulting and questions.

Vendor Contact

Dave Frey – MS-30
CareerTrack, Inc.
3085 Center Green Drive
Boulder, CO 80301-5408
VOICE   (800) 325-1202
FAX   (800) 685-7005

Checklist of Skills for Advanced High Performance Manufacturing

Description

This tool is a four-page checklist of skills that manufacturing personnel in high performance manufacturing industries must have. The checklist is divided into the following areas: communication and teamwork, match and measurement, workplace safety and health, problem solving, quality assurance, blueprint reading, manufacturing fundamentals, business planning and operation, computer use, product and process control, workforce issues, workplace skills and learning skills. The list, created through the input of high-performance manufacturers and educators, has been validated by industry and represents the skills and knowledge that industry needs of its workforce.

How Do I Use It?

Employers would use the checklist to evaluate prospective employees and create training programs.

Cost

Free.

Strengths and Weaknesses for Users

The list is a comprehensive yet concise listing of skills necessary for today's manufacturing environment. The conciseness can also be seen as a weakness in that an explanation or description of the skills is not included. However, the language of the checklist is very easily understood.

User Base

Not available.

User Support

	N/A	Available	Comments
Consultants	x		
Documentation		x	

	N/A	Available	Comments
Training Classes	x		
Telephone Support	x		

VENDOR CONTACT

The National Coalition for Advanced Manufacturing
1331 Pennsylvania, NW
Suite 1410—North Tower
Washington, DC 20004-1703
VOICE   (202) 662-8960
FAX   (202) 662-8964

CUSTOMER SERVICE INVENTORY (CSI)

DESCRIPTION

The PDI *Customer Service Inventory (CSI)* is a 64-item, paper-and-pencil questionnaire that is used to predict which job applicants are likely to provide friendly, helpful customer service. The *CSI* is appropriate for jobs in which successful performance consists primarily of building relationships and helping customers while remaining cheerful and positive. These are often hourly or entry-level jobs. Used as a consistent part of a hiring process, the *CSI* helps employers build a more customer-service-oriented workforce.

HOW DO I USE IT?

Employers give the *CSI* to job applicants (typically after an initial screening but before the interview) and use the scores along with the information from the application and interview to make final hiring decisions. Administration, scoring, and interpretation are quick and easy. Job applicants take about 10 minutes to complete the inventory. The *CSI* is scored on a convenient personal computer scoring disk, which takes about three minutes.

COST

The price of the *CSI* is based on the quantity used annually in a given company. Typically two to three inventories are given per job opening. A packet of 25 Inventory questionnaires costs $6.25. A packet of 50 costs $12.50. Scoring disks are available with five, 10, 25, or 50 scorings per disk. The *CSI* is also available in a 145-item version combined with the *PDI Employment Inventory* (EI) (see separate description of this tool on page 25).

Disk cost:

	CSI	Combined version
50 or fewer scorings annually	$13 per scoring	$17 per scoring
50-499 scorings annually	$12 per scoring	$16 per scoring

	CSI	Combined version
505-999 scorings annually	$11 per scoring	$15 per scoring
1000-2995 scorings annually	$10 per scoring	$14 per scoring

Additional price breaks available from vendor.

STRENGTHS AND WEAKNESSES FOR USERS

The *CSI* was developed by Personnel Decisions International (PDI), a leading consulting firm specializing in employee assessment. *CSI* scores have predicted employer and customer ratings of good customer service and sales data in over 40 validation studies. PDI provides free job analysis and training and consultants are available to answer implementation questions.

USER BASE

Over 15 million job applicants are screened annually with the *CSI* or *EI*. Users include major U.S. retailers, medical centers, airlines, restaurants, insurance companies, financial institutions, temporary employee agencies, car rental agencies and grocery stores. Typical jobs for which the *CSI* is used include customer service representative, clerk, sales associate, teller, nurse's aide, orderly, counter person, waiter, waitress, secretary, and help desk.

USER SUPPORT

	N/A	Available	Comments
Consultants		x	
Documentation		x	Use includes a free job analysis to confirm that the characteristics measured by the *CSI* are job-related.
Training Classes		x	
Telephone Support		x	

VENDOR CONTACT

Gina Less, Test Consultant
Personnel Decisions, Inc.
2000 Plaza VII Tower
45 South 7th Street
Minneapolis, MN 55402
VOICE   (612) 339-0927
FAX   (612) 337-8292

PDI also has offices in Dallas, Washington, DC, and Atlanta.

CUTTING EDGE TEAMWORK

DESCRIPTION

This tool is a video on self-managing teams. The subject is a high-tech company that has implemented self-management and teamwork. It presents the workers' perspective on new ways of working. It discusses the new role of supervisors and managers as coaches rather than overseers of work. It presents examples of schedule-setting, the role of team meetings, and critical issues such as information channels and business reviews. It also discusses the implementation of just-in-time processes.

HOW DO I USE IT?

The video could be used to facilitate a discussion among workers and management about how to structure self-managing teams. It could also be used in a company where teamwork is already underway to examine whether or not it is working. The video runs 12 minutes.

COST

The cost is $95 to rent and $395 to purchase. The rental period is five days. Videos may be previewed at no charge.

STRENGTHS AND WEAKNESSES FOR USERS

This is a very brief introduction to the teamwork concept for companies considering reorganizing work. It could apply in general to any work environment but relates specifically to a high-tech company.

USER BASE

Users of this tool include business, government, and education.

USER SUPPORT

	N/A	Available	Comments
Consultants	x		
Documentation	x		
Training Classes	x		
Telephone Support	x		

CRM Films has a complete catalog of training videos and will send it on request. Topics include appraising performance, managing diversity, and conducting interviews.

VENDOR CONTACT

CRM Films
2215 Faraday Avenue
Carlsbad, CA 92008-7295
VOICE (619) 431-9800
  (800) 421-0833
FAX (619) 931-5792

EMPLOYEE BENEFITS SURVEY 1993

DESCRIPTION

The survey gives comparative data on employee benefits in the plastics industry. Information includes vacation and holiday practices, sick leave, personal leave, disability, and much more.

HOW DO I USE IT?

Results are broken down by region, sales volume, and number of employees.

COST

Members of the Society of the Plastics Industry, $125; non-members, $250.

STRENGTHS AND WEAKNESSES FOR USERS

This is a comprehensive view of benefits data for the industry. Results are segmented for appropriate comparisons across similar companies in the same region.

USER BASE

Not Available.

USER SUPPORT

	N/A	Available	Comments
Consultants	x		
Documentation		x	
Training Classes	x		
Telephone Support		x	

VENDOR CONTACT

The Society of the Plastics Industry, Inc.
1275 K Street, NW, #400
Washington, DC 20005-4006
VOICE   (202) 371-5293

EMPLOYEE HANDBOOK OF NEW WORK HABITS FOR A RADICALLY CHANGING WORLD

DESCRIPTION

The Employee Handbook of New Work Habits For A Radically Changing World is the wake-up call needed by employees everywhere. Using hard facts and powerful logic, it literally corners the reader with the reality of how he or she must change because of the radical shifts in the world around us. This concise handbook gives employees the 13 ground rules to follow for success in the days ahead.

How Do I Use It?

This powerful tool is quick reading; there's no mushy theory or time-wasting trivia. *New Work Habits For A Radically Changing World* is a best-selling handbook that can be used both as a learning tool and a quick reference guide during times of change.

Cost

Each handbook costs $5.95 (quantity discounts available).

Strengths and Weaknesses for Users

The rapid shift to an entirely new economy, including vastly different approaches to the way organizations operate, presents many challenges. For those of us who embrace and play by the new rules, position themselves well, and take personal responsibility for their own future, the future offers many opportunities. Price Pritchett's best-selling handbook helps employees achieve and act upon that understanding.

User Base

Pritchett & Associates handbooks and training programs are used by more than 25,000 companies and close to 3,000,000 employees to exploit change for their competitive advantage.

User Support

	N/A	Available	Comments
Consultants		x	
Documentation		x	
Training Classes		x	
Telephone Support		x	

Vendor Contact

Pritchett & Associates, Inc.
13155 Noel Rd., Suite 1600
Dallas, TX 75240
VOICE   (800) 832-6434
FAX   (214) 789-7900

Employment Inventory (EI)

Description

The *PDI Employment Inventory (EI)* is a 97-item, paper-and-pencil questionnaire that is used to predict which job applicants are likely to be productive, dependable employees. The *EI* is appropriate for jobs in which successful performance consists primarily of showing up on time; following rules, directions and company procedures; and working carefully, methodically and steadily. These are typically hourly or entry-level jobs. Used as a consistent part of a hiring process, the *EI* helps employers build a better workforce.

How Do I Use It?

Employers give the *EI* to job applicants (typically after an initial screening but before the interview) and use the scores along with the information from the application and interview to make final hiring decisions. Administration, scoring, and interpretation are quick and easy. Job applicants take about 15 minutes to complete the inventory. The *EI* is scored on a convenient personal computer scoring disk, which takes about three minutes. Scores are easy to interpret to PDI's green-yellow-red guidelines.

Cost

The price of the *EI* is based on the quantity used annually in a given company. Typically two to three inventories are given per job opening. A packet of 25 Inventory questionnaires costs $6.25. A packet of 50 costs $12.50. Scoring disks are available with five, 10, 25, or 50 scorings per disk. The *EI* is also available in a 145-item version combined with the Customer Service Inventory (described as a separate tool above). Disk costs are as follows:

	EI	Combined version
50 or fewer scorings annually	$13 per scoring	$17 per scoring
50-499 scorings annually	$12 per scoring	$16 per scoring
505-999 scorings annually	$11 per scoring	$15 per scoring
1000-2995 scorings annually	$10 per scoring	$14 per scoring

Additional price breaks are available from the vendor.

Strengths and Weaknesses for Users

The *EI* was developed by Personnel Decisions International (PDI), a leading consulting firm that specializes in employee assessment. *EI* scores have predicted objective measures of job performance (such as turnover, accident rates, involuntary terminations, shrinkage and productivity) in over 150 validation studies. PDI provides free job analysis and training and consultants are available to answer implementation questions. The *EI* is available in English, English-Spanish, English-French.

User Base

Over 15 million job applicants are screened annually with the *EI* or CSI. Users include six of the top 10 retailers in the U.S., quick service restaurants, banks, gas stations, airlines, trucking lines, car rental agencies, grocery stores and manufacturers. Typical jobs for which the *EI* is used include the following: cashier, driver, sales clerk, sales associate, counter person, teller, production worker, baggage handler, stock clerk, security officer, and cook.

USER SUPPORT

	N/A	Available	Comments
Consultants		x	
Documentation		x	Use includes a free job analysis to confirm that the characteristics measured by the EI are job-related.
Training Classes		x	
Telephone Support		x	For clients who do not have personal computer scoring capability, PDI provides a phone scoring service.

VENDOR CONTACT

Gina Less, Test Consultant
Personnel Decisions, Inc.
2000 Plaza VII Tower
45 South 7th Street
Minneapolis, MN 55402
VOICE   (612) 339-0927
FAX   (612) 337-8292

PDI also has offices in Dallas, Washington, DC, and Atlanta.

EMPLOYEE OPINION SURVEY

DESCRIPTION

The *Employee Opinion Survey (EOS)* is best used as part of a company-wide diagnostic assessment process or as a stand-alone assessment of employee concerns. It is designed to solicit three types of data: demographic, qualitative, and quantitative. The first section of the *EOS* asks employees to complete statements concerning themselves. The second section of the questionnaire is designed to see how employees view their Quality of Worklife (QWL). Seven aspects of QWL are addressed: general satisfaction; policies, procedures and working conditions; communication and teamwork; pay and benefits; training and development; management effectiveness; and supervisory effectiveness. The third section consists of open-ended statements designed to cover any issues that the scaled items do not address.

HOW DO I USE IT?

The *EOS* tool comes with a process manual and questionnaires. The survey process should be administered by a neutral service-provider team. The team works at the company site to guide management, administer written surveys, and interview employees. The service-provider team enters the survey data into a statistical software package for analysis and cross-tabulation. Company management, with assistance from the *EOS* team, can formulate an action plan to address the results of the survey.

COST

The *EOS* manual and employee survey forms are available for $290. Data analysis requires spreadsheet and statistical software that are not included. Individual consultation on use of the *EOS* tool and follow-up phone support are provided on a fee basis if staff are available.

STRENGTHS AND WEAKNESSES FOR USERS

The questionnaire provides good feedback about the overall culture of the company for company management. The quantitative and qualitative data can be stored by different demographic groups to better pinpoint areas of the company that need improvement.

The user or service provider should be clear about what the company wants to know and alter the survey questions to collect the needed data. The service provider needs to assure the employees that their responses are confidential. To get maximum benefit, the questions should be analyzed with a statistical software package so certain questions can be cross referenced to jobs, departments, shifts, etc. Therefore, possession of and proficiency in the software package are important.

Interpreting the results and developing a company action plan are the most important aspects of the engagement. These latter steps require experience and skill on the part of the service provider and are not inherent in the tool.

USER BASE

The survey has been used in approximately 50 companies throughout the Southeast. It was first developed in 1986 and has been used by three technical assistance programs at Georgia Tech. Each program has modified the survey process to meet a particular program focus.

USER SUPPORT

	N/A	Available	Comments
Consultants		x	Georgia Tech staff available to instruct users on a fee basis.
Documentation		x	Comes with procedure handbook and employee questionnaires.
Training Classes	x		Not available at this time.
Telephone Support		x	Georgia Tech staff available on a fee basis.

VENDOR CONTACT

Vicki Bryan
Information and Data Services
Economic Development Institute
Georgia Institute of Technology
222 O'Keefe Building

Atlanta, GA 30332
VOICE   (404) 894-4263
FAX   (404) 853-9172
E-MAIL   vicki.bryan@edi.gatech.edu

EVERYBODY LEADS

DESCRIPTION

This tool is a two-part video on working in teams. The subject is a plastic resin processing company that has redesigned its organization around self-management and teamwork. The team members talk about self-management and how their jobs have changed. It discusses the new role of foreman and the concept of rotating leadership. It presents examples of processes for job rotation, empowerment, interdependence, decision-making, and quality control. The video concludes with a summary of the results in quality improvement and productivity that have been achieved.

HOW DO I USE IT?

The video could be used to facilitate a discussion among workers and management about the prospect of moving to teams operating with self-leadership. It could also be used in a company where teamwork is already being tried to examine whether or not it is working. The video comes in two parts: the first part is 15 minutes; the second part runs 13 minutes.

COST

The videos cost $95 to rent and $395 to purchase. The rental period is five days. Videos may be previewed at no charge.

STRENGTHS AND WEAKNESSES FOR USERS

This video takes the teamwork concept and illustrates what it actually means for how people do their jobs. It does not provide specifics on how to implement any of these changes. It is useful for showing the benefits of teamwork and self-leadership to those who might be unaware of the concept or skeptical about it.

USER BASE

Business, government, and education.

USER SUPPORT

	N/A	Available	Comments
Consultants	x		
Documentation	x		
Training Classes	x		
Telephone Support	x		

CRM Films has a complete catalog of training videos and will send it on request. Topics include appraising performance, managing diversity, and conducting interviews.

VENDOR CONTACT

CRM Films
2215 Faraday Avenue
Carlsbad, CA 92008-7295
VOICE (619) 431-9800
       (800) 421-0833
FAX   (619) 931-5792

HOW TO CREATE AND DELIVER A DYNAMIC PRESENTATION

DESCRIPTION

How to Create and Deliver a Dynamic Presentation by Doug Malouf gives readers an entertaining and thorough tour of presentation principles. Topics include preparation techniques, icebreakers, reinforcement, visual aids and common mistakes. User-friendly and humorously illustrated, Malouf's book provides practical suggestions from a presentation expert.

HOW DO I USE IT?

Extremely easy to read and quite funny, *How to Create and Deliver a Dynamic Presentation* covers all aspects of public speaking from the ideal physical layout of the room to the use of humor. Readers can review specific topics, pick up a number of practical aids and games, or read all of the book to get Malouf's unique perspective on presentation skills.

COST

This book is available to ASTD members for $22 and to non-members for $25.

STRENGTHS AND WEAKNESSES FOR USERS

The enthusiasm needed in any public presentation is readily apparent in Malouf's writing. *How to Create and Deliver a Dynamic Presentation* reads like an actual presentation, complete with visual aids and humor. The information is both specific and based on the author's own vast experience. The only warning? Overly serious or theoretically minded persons may be put off by Malouf's informal style. Everyone else will find an easy-to-handle resource for a nerve-rattling subject.

USER BASE

Not available.

USER SUPPORT

	N/A	Available	Comments
Consultants	x		
Documentation	x		
Training Classes	x		
Telephone Support	x		

VENDOR CONTACT

ASTD Publishing Service
Priority Code IDT
P.O. Box 4856, Hampden Station
Baltimore, MD 21211

HUMAN RESOURCES ASSESSMENT PROTOCOL (HRAP)

DESCRIPTION

The Great Lakes Manufacturing Technology Center's (GLMTC) *Human Resource Assessment Protocol (HRAP)* is designed to assist manufacturers in adopting positive "people practices" consistent with high performance organizations. Specifically, in two or three days on-site, consultants will investigate both management's and workers' perceptions to determine areas for improvement in seven major domains:

- Management and leadership;
- Communications;
- Education and training needs;
- Empowerment;
- Recognition/rewards and compensation/benefits;
- Safety and health perceptions; and
- Employee knowledge of customer wants and needs.

HOW DO I USE IT?

The assessment consists of one half-day of interviews with key company executives so that the assessment team may obtain a "top-down" view of company goals and challenges. At this time, the team will also review their findings with management and leave a Company Information form to be filled out. At a mutually convenient time, the team will spend two days on-site. During that visit the assessment team will interview all of the managers and supervisors for approximately one hour each. In addition, one-hour focus group discussions (typically 8-15 people each) will be held with most, if not all of the non-management employees. Groups are designed so that employees feel free to share their issues and concerns with the assessment team.

A questionnaire is also provided to all employees as a part of obtaining their perceptions about different aspects of the organization. These questionnaires are separated into three sets:

- All employees;
- Managers/supervisors; and
- Non-management personnel.

The GLMTC assessment team provides the customer company a written report that describes how the company may improve its human resource utilization. In the report, the assessment team explains the data collected, deduces some probable causes for observed situations, and provides specific recommendations for company follow-up. These recommendations also point out where current practices may be inconsistent with those of high performing organizations.

COST

The GLMTC will charge clients $1,750 per day on-site. Organizations with 50-150 employees usually require a two-to-three-day Assessment.

STRENGTHS AND WEAKNESSES FOR USERS

The *HRAP* provides a relatively quick and inexpensive approach to assessing "people practices" or human resources within manufacturing organizations. The *HRAP* provides a very detailed and widespread internal view of all of the activities within an organization that are affected by their employees. This tool also helps improve competitiveness to the small and medium-sized manufacturer by comparing current HR efforts to that of high performance organizations.

The data collection and analysis can be very time-consuming. On average, the GLMTC staff spends 60-90 hours on each *HRAP* (based on a two-to-three-day Assessment). *HRAP* assessors must go through an initial training session in the use of the tool. Some background in Human Resources is also necessary to provide the assessment and organizational development skills needed. Because this tool can analyze employees' perceptions regarding every aspect of the organization, some knowledge or experience of the manufacturing process is helpful.

USER BASE

Although the GLMTC designed *HRAP* specifically for manufacturing firms employing 50 to 150 workers in the fabricated metal products and industrial machinery and equipment industries, the tool has been used in several areas of manufacturing. Teams from the Manufacturing Technology Centers (MTC) have conducted human resource assessments for nine firms.

USER SUPPORT

	N/A	Available	Comments
Consultants	x		
Documentation		x	
Training Classes		x	MTC staff must receive training to use the *HRAP* tool. The center offers one or two-day training sessions as needed

N/A	Available	Comments
		for staff from MTCs and anyone else who might benefit from use of the tool.
Telephone Support x		

VENDOR CONTACT

Steven C. Crimaldi
Human Resource Program Associate
Great Lakes Manufacturing Technology Center
4600 Prospect Avenue
Cleveland, Ohio 44103-4314
VOICE   (216) 432-5396
FAX   (216) 432-5314
E-MAIL   steven.crimaldi@camp.org

INFO-LINE

DESCRIPTION

Info-Line is a monthly monograph on a topic of interest to trainers and other human resource professionals. The monthly publication ranges from 16 to 20 pages of easy-to-read materials from experts in the training field, accompanied by charts, checklists, diagrams, bibliographies, and a copyright-free job aid. Issues of interest include:

- First-Rate Technical & Skills Training;
- Basic Training for Trainers;
- Diagnostic Tools for Total Quality;
- Continuous Process Improvement;
- Alternatives to Lecture;
- How to Produce Great Job Aids;
- Get Results with the Case Method;
- Job Related Literacy: Teaching Reading on the Job;
- Basics of Instructional Systems Development;
- Course Design and Development; and
- Workforce Education.

HOW DO I USE IT?

Readers use *Info-Line* for a variety of reasons, ranging from improving their personal training skills to designing course materials to keeping it as a ready reference on a variety of topics. It is a monthly series.

COST

Info-Line is available through yearly subscription ($119 for 12 issues) or by single issue ($10 each, plus $2.50 shipping and handling). Bulk rates for single issues apply.

STRENGTHS AND WEAKNESSES FOR USERS

Info-Line provides overviews and how-to information on training topics. Readers find the format useful and easy to digest. Given the length of the periodical, most topics cannot be covered in-depth. However, the publication provides bibliographies showing where individuals can go for more information.

The program does not specifically focus on metalworking firms, though it will be of use to them.

USER BASE

Not available.

USER SUPPORT

	N/A	Available	Comments
Consultants	x		
Documentation	x		
Training Classes	x		
Telephone Support	x		

VENDOR CONTACT

ASTD Fulfillment
Priority Code IDT
P.O. Box 1567
Merrifield, VA 22116-1567
Phone orders: (703) 683-8100 and use priority code IDT.

INTEGRATING TECHNOLOGY WITH WORKERS IN THE NEW AMERICAN WORKPLACE

DESCRIPTION

Integrating Technology with Workers in the New American Workplace is a 1994 report from the U.S. Department of Labor's Office of the American Workplace. The study is founded on the notion that success in the workplace may depend less on available hardware and software than on effective utilization of technology among employees. The report looks at how technology is affecting workers and their workplaces and which technology practices are most effective.

How Do I Use It?

The study is organized into nine sections, including: Introduction; Workers in the Technology Revolution; Organizations in the Technology Revolution; Getting the Most from New Technology; Technology Practice 1—Training Workers to Use Technology; Technology Practice 2—Giving Workers Control of Technology; Technology Practice 3—Involving Workers in Technology Design and Implementation; and Investing in Workers and Technologies for More Effective Organizations. Nine case studies are examined, including studies of Fannie Mae and the Boeing 777.

Cost

Integrating Technology with Workers in the New American Workplace is available for $5 per copy.

Strengths and Weaknesses for Users

The report makes good use of case histories to help the user identify "success stories" of integrating technology into the workplace. It also includes an 11-page reference section. The report is 77 pages long.

User Base

Not available.

User Support

	N/A	Available	Comments
Consultants	x		
Documentation		x	
Training Classes	x		
Telephone Support	x		

Vendor Contact

Office of the American Workplace
U.S. Department of Labor
Washington, DC 20210
VOICE   (202) 512-1800
FAX   (202) 219-8762

Is Training for You?

Description

This 18-minute videotape carries an important message for top management—specifically, that a company's strategy for survival and growth must include continuous employee training. Employee training—done right—consists of an effective, well-organized effort with full management backing. This tape is a must for safety and training directors looking to convince upper management of the need to invest in employee training programs.

How Do I Use It?

The videotape plays in standard VHS format. The tape explains the importance of training to any metalforming organization.

Cost

This videotape is free to members of the Precision Metalforming Association, but costs $25 for the general public.

Strengths and Weaknesses for Users

This videotape addresses one of the basic challenges in training. It explains that training, while traditionally viewed as a cost of operations, is actually an important investment in the company's future. It helps justify training programs to upper management while persuading them of training's value. It also stresses the importance of management commitment to any successful training program. The videotape focuses exclusively on this issue.

User Base

The Precision Metalforming Association represents the $31 billion metalforming industry of North America—the industry that gives utility to sheet metal by shaping it using tooling machines. The membership consists of more than 1,300 companies including metal stampers, fabricators, spinners, and roll formers, as well as suppliers of equipment, materials, and services to the industry.

User Support

	N/A	Available	Comments
Consultants	x		
Documentation	x		
Training Classes	x		
Telephone Support	x		

Vendor Contact

The Precision Metalforming Association
27027 Chardon Road
Richmond Heights, OH 44143
VOICE   (216) 585-8800
FAX   (216) 585-3126

LABOR SURVEY 1994/
SALARY AND SALES POLICY SURVEY 1994

DESCRIPTION

These two reports give detailed information of wages paid within the plastics industry, as gathered from hundreds of companies. Hourly rates are included for 62 job classifications. Salaries are given for front-line supervisors and 39 professionals within the industry.

HOW DO I USE IT?

Information is provided by size, region and occupation.

COST

Members of the Society of the Plastics Industry, $100; non-members, $200

STRENGTHS AND WEAKNESSES FOR USERS

The surveys provide data from real facilities in the industry for industry-specific occupations. Data is segmented by sales volume and region.

USER BASE

Not available.

USER SUPPORT

	N/A	Available	Comments
Consultants	x		
Documentation		x	
Training Classes	x		
Telephone Support		x	

VENDOR CONTACT

The Society of the Plastics Industry, Inc.
1275 K Street, NW, #400
Washington, DC 20005-4006
VOICE   (202) 371-5293

LITERATURE CATALOGUE 1995-1996— THE SOCIETY OF THE PLASTICS INDUSTRY, INC.

DESCRIPTION

This catalog lists all the publications produced by the Society of Plastics Industry, a membership organization of the Plastics Industry. It contains information about many areas important to the industry: environment, general business practices, and sector-specific reports.

HOW DO I USE IT?

The catalog is divided into specific areas of interest: membership, general reference, industry mobilization, energy, environment and safety. Many industry sectors also have additional listings of technical reports on topics such as sheet products or vinyl siding. Reports can be ordered using an 800-number or a mail order form.

COST

Costs vary by report. Non-members of the Society of Plastics Industry are always charged more than members.

STRENGTHS AND WEAKNESSES FOR USERS

The catalog is an extensive resource that provides information on general industry as well as sector-specific information about the plastics industry.

USER BASE

Not available.

USER SUPPORT

	N/A	Available	Comments
Consultants	x		
Documentation		x	
Training Classes	x		
Telephone Support		x	

VENDOR CONTACT

The Society of the Plastics Industry, Inc.
1275 K Street, NW, #400
Washington, DC 20005-4006
VOICE   (202) 371-5332

METALWORKING SKILLS STANDARDS

DESCRIPTION

The metalworking skills standards are performance-based standards for duties, tasks, knowledge, skills, abilities, and other characteristics of skilled metalworking occupations. Three levels of *Machining Skills Standards* have been published. Standards also are under development for specialties in metalforming, machine building and maintenance, and tool making. The standards are developed with broad-based participation from business, labor, and education representatives.

HOW DO I USE IT?

The standards allow employers to assess needs for training and education among existing and prospective employees. The standards can also be used to develop customized curricula for training and education programs, or in support of apprenticeships or other work-based learning programs.

COST

Level I, II, and III *Machining Skills Standards* are available from NTMA at $24.95 each.

STRENGTHS AND WEAKNESSES FOR USERS

The standards provide the first competency-based assessment benchmarks for precision metalworking occupations. A formal system of testing and certification is not available at present but is under development.

USER BASE

Employers, employees and providers of education and training.

USER SUPPORT

	N/A	Available	Comments
Consultants		x	Available on a limited basis. Inquire with NTMA.
Documentation		x	
Training Classes		x	Can be established locally.
Telephone Support	x		

VENDOR CONTACT

The National Tooling & Machining Association
9300 Livingston Road
Ft. Washington, MD 20744
VOICE   (301) 248-6200
FAX   (301) 248-7104

Metalworking Training System

Description

This product is the first fully structured program for teaching metalworking technology. The National Tooling & Machining Association's (NTMA) customized, ready-made training system provides state-of-the-art training programs for metalworking firms. These unique training materials help companies improve their training programs. The first program in this system is a complete turnkey package that prepares employees for careers as machinists and other precision metalworking specialties. The objective of the system is to bring a company's training program up to the standards of excellence demanded by America's dynamic metalworking industry. The program addresses training needs in such metalworking professions as machinists, moldmakers, diemakers, toolmakers, manufacturing work cell technicians, CIM technicians, flexible manufacturing specialists, and N/C operators.

Areas covered by the modules include basic machine setups and operations, intermediate machining technology, advanced machining technology, benchwork, shop math, blueprint, first aid and other related technology areas.

How Do I Use It?

The 320 teaching modules form the backbone of the training system. Each module covers specific job-related task objectives. Companies can follow the modules in order or can pick and choose specific modules according to their needs.

Cost

The cost of each module is $7.50. The total package of 320 modules is $1,920. This tool is available only to NTMA members.

Strengths and Weaknesses for Users

Because the product consists of a training program, it can be used repeatedly for many employees. It is not just a canned training program; it embodies a train-the-trainer philosophy to increase the effectiveness of a company's entire training efforts.

User Base

NTMA consists of more than 3,000 tooling and machining companies in 56 chapters throughout the U.S. Sixty-five percent of the members have 20 employees or less.

User Support

	N/A	Available	Comments
Consultants	x		
Documentation		x	
Training Classes		x	
Telephone Support		x	

The National Tooling & Machining Association
9300 Livingston Road
Ft. Washington, MD 20744
VOICE   (301) 248-6200
FAX   (301) 248-7104

Minor Laws of Major Importance

Description

Minor Laws of Major Importance, compiled by the Academy for Educational Development's National Institute for Work and Learning, is the first source book of its kind which explicitly states the federal and state legislation that affects workers under the age of 18.

How Do I Use It?

Broken down by state, *Minor Laws of Major Importance* provides names and telephone numbers of Labor/Employment Agencies and lists state laws regarding teenagers 14-17 years of age, night work restrictions and other specific regulations.

Cost

The cost is $10.95 plus $4 shipping and handling for the first book and $.50 for each additional copy. Quantity discounts are available for 10 or more copies (20 percent) and 50 or more copies (40 percent).

Strengths and Weaknesses for Users

This book offers a comprehensive resource for those interested in labor laws.

User Base

School personnel, parents, employers and community-based organizations will find *Minor Laws of Major Importance* useful in explaining those labor laws.

User Support

	N/A	Available	Comments
Consultants	x		
Documentation	x		
Training Classes	x		
Telephone Support	x		

Vendor Contact

Kendall/Hunt Publishing Company
4050 Westmark Drive

P.O. Box 1840
Dubuque, IA 52004-1840
VOICE   (800) 228-0810
FAX   (800) 772-9165

NATIONAL OCCUPATIONAL SKILL STANDARDS FOR CADD

DESCRIPTION

The Foundation for Industrial Modernization has developed national, voluntary skill standards for computer-aided drafting and design users. The skills will be used to develop a national certification program. Skill standards are intended to help industry by improving the skills of the workforce. They also assist educators and trainers in curriculum development and ensure that students and workers develop skills necessary for employment in the industry.

HOW DO I USE IT?

For employers, the skills document can be used as criteria for hiring, evaluating job performance, and determining retraining needs. For employees, the document can provide a list of skills needed to stay current, skills necessary for national certification, and core skills portable across CADD disciplines.

COST

$22.50 per copy.

STRENGTHS AND WEAKNESSES FOR USERS

The standards were developed by a coalition from industry, education, and labor. They were reviewed by over 200 CADD user organizations.

USER BASE

Not available.

USER SUPPORT

	N/A	Available	Comments
Consultants	x		
Documentation		x	
Training Classes	x		
Telephone Support	x		

VENDOR CONTACT

The National Coalition for Advanced Manufacturing (NACFAM)
1331 Pennsylvania, NW
Suite 1410 – North Tower

Washington, DC 20004-1703
VOICE   (202) 662-8960
FAX   (202) 662-8964

NCTPC TRAINING PROGRAMS COURSE SCHEDULE CATALOG

DESCRIPTION

The National Center for Tooling & Precision Components (NCTPC) is a nonprofit organization that provides programs to improve the competitive positions of U.S. tooling and manufacturing companies. The programs involve training and education; technical and business assistance; and research and development. Training activities include a broad range of scheduled classes ranging from Unix and personal computer-based CAD/CAM, ISO 9000, and Materials and Strain Analysis to Metrology and Rapid Prototyping.

The NCTPC also develops custom training programs to address companies' specific problems and needs.

HOW DO I USE IT?

This 14-page catalog is indexed by category. It includes schedule dates, costs, and registration information as well as instructions on whom to contact for custom training programs.

COST

Varies depending on training program.

STRENGTHS AND WEAKNESSES FOR USERS

The NCTPC programs cover a broad range of topics on a variety of levels, thus accommodating a range of users from beginners through experienced, advanced employees. The NCTPC serves companies from the smallest shops to global corporations.

USER BASE

Not available.

USER SUPPORT

	N/A	Available	Comments
Consultants		x	
Documentation	x		
Training Classes		x	
Telephone Support		x	

VENDOR CONTACT

NCTPC
National Center for Tooling & Precision Components
2600 Dorr Street
Toledo, OH 43607-3237
VOICE   (419) 531-8340 or
           (800) 996-2872
FAX   (419) 531-8412

NATIONAL TOOLING & MACHINING ASSOCIATION (NTMA) PUBLICATION AND TRAINING MATERIALS CATALOG

DESCRIPTION

This tool represents the best collection of training and information resources specifically designed for the tooling and machining industry. It is divided into three sections: materials for metalworking trainees, materials for industry shop owners and managers, and audio-visual materials that focus on both segments. Information about customized training programs offered by NTMA is also included.

HOW DO I USE IT?

Short descriptions of each course or publication are classified by one of the three broad subject areas described above. Once a set of materials captures the user's interest, the user contacts NTMA for more information or to order the product.

COST

Cost of the materials depends upon the specific program. To members, prices range from $6 to more than $300. Although some products cost the same for all buyers, non-members usually will be charged 50 percent more than NTMA members.

STRENGTHS AND WEAKNESSES FOR USERS

Because of NTMA's specialization, these training materials provide the best focused training of tool and die employees on the market. Also, NTMA's 30-year history of providing and testing training materials means its training programs are of the highest caliber. The materials are reasonably priced, and the catalog descriptions are informative.   Ordering instructions and customer support seem clear and helpful.

USER BASE

NTMA consists of more than 3,000 tooling and machining companies in 56 chapters throughout the U.S. Sixty-five percent of the members have 20 employees or less. Many schools use NTMA's materials for vocational technology or metalworking technology courses.

USER SUPPORT

	N/A	Available	Comments
Consultants	x		
Documentation		x	
Training Classes		x	
Telephone Support		x	

VENDOR CONTACT

The National Tooling & Machining Association
9300 Livingston Road
Ft. Washington, MD 20744
VOICE   (301) 248-6200
FAX   (301) 248-7104

OPQ & ABILITY TESTING

DESCRIPTION

This Saville & Holdsworth, Ltd. assessment system contains more than 50 different work-relevant personal style and ability measures. The measures can be combined into regimes for selection, placement, and career development activities. Output formats include profile sheets, Expert System interpretative reports, and Candidate Match reports which compare individual score patterns to the attribute requirements of any job described by the Saville & Holdsworth Ltd. *Work Profiling System* (see the description of this tool on page 57).

HOW DO I USE IT?

Assessments are available in paper and pencil format or via computer administration. Answer sheets can be hand-scored or computer-scored in-house or may be sent to Saville & Holdsworth for scoring and interpretive reports.

COST

Assessment pricing is based on choice of paper and pencil or computer administration formats. Reusable administration booklets range from $20 to $27.50. Answer sheets average $7.50 each including scoring. Computer administrations average $15 each. Expert System interpretive reports and Candidate Match reports cost between $25 and $75 per person. In-house software packages and volume discounts are available.

STRENGTHS AND WEAKNESSES FOR USERS

Most of the personal style and ability measures can be administered, scored, and interpreted using an integrated computer system. Individual candidate performance can be matched against profiles of many different jobs. Use of some personality measures requires certification from Saville & Holdsworth.

Any employee can be tested and evaluated against their current position or they can be compared to the requirements of other positions within the organization to find the best match.

USER BASE

Over 20,000 organizations in 30 countries use Saville & Holdsworth assessment materials. United States users include AT&T, Kodak, and Proctor & Gamble.

USER SUPPORT

	N/A	Available	Comments
Consultants		x	
Documentation	x		
Training Classes	x		
Telephone Support		x	

VENDOR CONTACT

Saville & Holdsworth Ltd.
575 Boylston Street
Boston, MA 02116
VOICE   (800) 899-7451

PERSONNEL PROFILING

DESCRIPTION

Personnel Profiling, a product of Resource Associates, Inc., helps employers select candidates who are higher in productivity, more quality-minded, and better able to get along with people. This is a pre-employment test battery that measures important job-related aptitudes (e.g., abstract reasoning, mechanical comprehension, spatial aptitude and mathematical ability), and personality characteristics (e.g., teamwork, conscientiousness, work drive and ability to handle pressure). The Personnel Profiling system can also help lower turnover and absenteeism as well as identify potential problem areas. It has been validated in a wide range of manufacturing settings, including among general production workers, fabricators, assemblers, welders, forgers, machinists, press operators, utility workers, inspectors, and benchworkers.

HOW DO I USE IT?

The user administers the *Personnel Profiling* test battery to candidates for job openings. Next, answer sheets are transmitted to Resource Associates by mail, FAX or overnight shipping service. Test results are provided to the user in less than 24 hours, usually overnight by FAX. To help tailor the battery to a specific situation, the user must first complete a brief job analysis and specification form. A test battery and administration guide will be supplied to the user. Test administration procedures will be reviewed with Resource Associates by phone prior to usage.

Cost

Personnel Profiling has a flat cost of $25 per applicant tested and scored. There is no charge for the job analysis and test-administrator orientation. There is a one-time materials cost of $75. Users can photocopy Resource Associates' tests and forms by permission.

Strengths and Weaknesses for Users

The pre-employment test batteries have been used successfully in many different jobs in many different manufacturing, distribution, and service settings. The batteries are reliable, valid, and standardized. They also meet EEO and ADA guidelines. Licensed industrial-organizational psychologists administer the *Personnel Profiling* program. The cost of this service will save significant expenses associated with recruitment, hiring, training, and turnover and may be recaptured many times over in increased work productivity and quality. The firm also maintains a database to store results and track applicant data over time for the user. The user must, in most cases, assume responsibility for on-site test administration, test security, and transmittal of answer sheets.

User Base

More than 100 companies in the Southeastern United States use these pre-employment test batteries to screen applicants for jobs.

User Support

	N/A	Available	Comments
Consultants		x	Ph.D.-level industrial-organizational psychologists available for ongoing technical assistance and consultation.
Documentation		x	Test Administrator's Manual provided. Examples of validity studies available.
Training Classes		x	Training classes available on request.
Telephone Support		x	Consultants available mornings, afternoons, and evenings seven days/wk.

Vendor Contact

Resource Associates, Inc.
5455 Lance Drive
Knoxville, TN 37909
Attn: John W. Lounsbury, Ph.D.
VOICE   (615) 588-8252
FAX   (615) 584-4252
E-MAIL   jlounsbury@aol.com

PRECISION MACHINING TECHNOLOGY (PMT) TRAINING PROGRAM

DESCRIPTION

The National Center for Tooling & Precision Components (NCTPC) is a nonprofit organization which provides programs in training and education; technical and business assistance; and research and development to improve the competitive positions of U.S. tooling and manufacturing companies. The *PMT* program is an intensive 29-week program that teaches the fundamental knowledge and skills that industry is demanding of employees going into entry-level positions in the machine trades. The program is half classroom and half hands-on training based on the guidelines published in the NTMA's new *Duties and Standards for Machining Skills* training manuals.

The NCTPC also conducts other training classes and programs, and develops and implements custom training programs to address companies' specific problems and needs.

HOW DO I USE IT?

A brochure describes the program's features and benefits as well as the benefits of building a career in the machine trades.

COST

Varies depending on training program.

STRENGTHS AND WEAKNESSES FOR USERS

The NCPTC serves companies from the smallest shops to global corporations.

USER BASE

Not available.

USER SUPPORT

	N/A	Available	Comments
Consultants		x	
Documentation	x		
Training Classes		x	
Telephone Support		x	

VENDOR CONTACT

NCTPC
National Center for Tooling & Precision Components
2600 Dorr Street
Toledo, OH 43607-3237
VOICE   (419) 531-8340 or

	(800) 996-2872
FAX	(419) 531-8412

PRESS BRAKE OPERATOR TRAINING

DESCRIPTION

This videotape training program teaches employees the fundamentals of press brake operation. Topics include machine usage, safety, startup and shutdown procedures, piece part production, measuring and inspecting, tooling, gaging, and setup and tear-down procedures. The complete training system includes easy-to-follow instructions, eight VHS tapes, three training manuals, one set of trainee worksheets, and certificates of completion.

HOW DO I USE IT?

Training is easy with the Precision Metalforming Association's (PMA) unique VIEW/ReVIEW Training Systems. They are unique self-paced learning programs that place the responsibility for learning on the individual employee and minimize interruptions. Training manuals lead employees through the operations described above. Worksheets promote practical usage and testing of information included in the tapes and text. With PMA video training systems, employees learn what they need to know in order to be safer and more productive. Refresher courses and new employee training are hassle-free because the training stays on-site.

COST

The first set of the system costs $2,400 for PMA members, with additional sets costing $400. The first set of the system costs $4,800 for the general public, with additional sets costing $800.

STRENGTHS AND WEAKNESSES FOR USERS

Users move at their own pace through the training materials. The system uses several media— VHS videotapes, written exercises, and text—to teach the course.

USER BASE

The Precision Metalforming Association represents the $31 billion metalforming industry of North America, which is the industry that gives utility to sheet metal by shaping it using tooling machines. The membership consists of more than 1,300 companies, including metal stampers, fabricators, spinners, and roll formers, as well as suppliers of equipment, materials and services to the industry.

USER SUPPORT

	N/A	Available	Comments
Consultants	x		
Documentation		x	
Training Classes	x		
Telephone Support	x		

VENDOR CONTACT

The Precision Metalforming Association
27027 Chardon Road
Richmond Heights, OH 44143
VOICE   (216) 585-8800
FAX   (216) 585-3126

ROAD TO HIGH PERFORMANCE WORKPLACES: A GUIDE TO BETTER JOBS AND BETTER BUSINESS RESULTS

DESCRIPTION

This 29-page booklet gives a company a broad approach to assessing its capacity to be a high-performance workplace. It provides summary text and a checklist of practices in each of the following areas: 1) skills and information; 2) participation, organization, and partnership; 3) compensation, security, and work environment; and 4) putting it all together. A reference guide is provided for additional reading.

HOW DO I USE IT?

Road to High Performance Workplaces is a well-organized, readable booklet that is structured by chapters and topic headings and includes a 33-item checklist. In each area, conceptual background and evidence for the utility of specific practices are presented.

COST

Road to High Performance Workplaces costs $2.50.

STRENGTHS AND WEAKNESSES FOR USERS

This is a useful overview and self-assessment for a company interested in transforming its organizational, managerial, and human resources practices. It can serve as a quick training or orientation tool. The lack of depth devoted to specific issues is a weakness, although references and additional information sources are identified.

USER BASE

This is a new publication.

USER SUPPORT

	N/A	Available	Comments
Consultants	x		
Documentation	x		
Training Classes	x		
Telephone Support	x		

VENDOR CONTACT
U.S. Dept. of Labor
Washington, DC 20210
VOICE   (202) 219-6045

To purchase copies, contact Superintendent of Documents at (202) 783-3238
Stock number: 029-000-00450-1

STRUCTURED ON-THE-JOB TRAINING: UNLEASHING EMPLOYEE EXPERTISE IN THE WORKPLACE

DESCRIPTION

Structured On-the-Job Training: Unleashing Employee Expertise in the Workplace provides a practical approach to design, deliver, and evaluate training programs conducted on the job. While practical in intent, the book is based on nearly a decade of research and development work in a variety of organizational settings.

The book is based on two key assumptions. First, the demands of the new economy, which include greater flexibility in production and service delivery, use of advanced technologies and greater responsiveness to the requirements of customers, have made employee expertise a strategic necessity. Second, new forms of on-the-job-training (OJT) in the past have been relatively unplanned and, thus, can be considered unstructured in nature.

HOW DO I USE IT?

This book is relatively self-standing in that it guides the reader through the steps of the structured OJT process. Numerous examples, checklists and comments are provided to help clarify the content. In addition, the authors would be available in a consulting role to help individual companies meet their specific needs. For example, the author offers a comprehensive training seminar to help experts become structured OJT trainers.

COST

The retail cost of the book is $29.95. Discounts are available when the book is used as part of author-led seminars.

STRENGTHS AND WEAKNESSES FOR USERS

Few books are available that provide comprehensive, up-to-date information about how to conduct training in the workplace. In addition, the book addresses how to use structured OJT for different types of training: technical, managerial, and awareness. Finally, the techniques and ideas presented in the book are based on extensive research and development experiences. However, the book is limited to structured OJT, and does not cover other in-depth forms of on-the-job learning opportunity. Also, to get the most from the content, it seems necessary for readers to have some knowledge and skills in human resource development.

USER BASE

The authors have implemented structured OJT in a variety of companies, including manufacturing, assembly, retail banking and financial services. The term "structured OJT" was originated by the author in 1987, who has since introduced it to human resource development professionals and managers in the United States as well as the Netherlands, Egypt, Mexico, Taiwan, and Singapore.

USER SUPPORT

	N/A	Available	Comments
Consultants	x		
Documentation	x		
Training Classes	x		
Telephone Support	x		

VENDOR CONTACT

Ronald L. Jacobs, Ph.D.
Professor, Human Resource Development
325 Ramseyer Hall
Ohio State University
Columbus, OH 43210
VOICE   (614) 292-5037
FAX   (614) 292-7812
E-MAIL   rjacobs@magnus.acs.ohio-state.edu

TECHNICAL & SKILLS TRAINING MAGAZINE

DESCRIPTION

Technical & Skills Training is written specifically to meet the unique needs of technical trainers—professionals who train managers, supervisors, and employees to use new technology. Every issue contains training techniques and tools for designing, delivering, and evaluating technical training.

HOW DO I USE IT?

People who subscribe to this magazine get practical, real-world information on technical training programs ranging from end-user computer training to metalworking apprenticeship programs to continuing education for engineers. The magazine also publishes a "News and Trends" column that presents short summaries of issues related to training and development. Readers also use the magazine for networking; it publishes the authors' addresses and phone numbers so readers can contact them for more information.

COST

Technical & Skills Training is published eight times a year. The annual subscription rate is $50 for ASTD members and $59 for non-members.

STRENGTHS AND WEAKNESSES

Technical & Skills Training is the only publication devoted to the fast-growing field of technical training. As more companies purchase technology—from robots, to computer-numerically controlled machines to laptop computers—employees need to be trained quickly and thoroughly to operate the technology. The magazine covers many industries and occupations, including metalworking, but all editorial material focuses on technical training. Articles are written in a user-friendly style with liberal use of charts, checklists, job aids, guidelines, and tips.

The program does not specifically focus on metalworking firms, though it will be of use to them.

USER BASE

Technical & Skills Training has approximately 9,000 subscribers and 27,000 readers. ASTD markets the magazine through worldwide direct-mail promotions and many targeted efforts to specific groups of technical trainers and industry sectors.

USER SUPPORT

	N/A	Available	Comments
Consultants	x		
Documentation	x		
Training Classes	x		
Telephone Support	x		

VENDOR CONTACT

Ellen Carnevale, Editor
Technical & Skills Training
American Society for Training and Development
1640 King St., Box 1443
Alexandria, VA 22313
(703) 683-8155

TQM AND ENVIRONMENTAL MANAGEMENT

DESCRIPTION

In this report, readers will gain the insights of top U.S., European, and Canadian quality and environmental executives as they look at environmental management from the quality perspective. This research study details how management can apply quality principles and practices—such as quality training, self-assessment, problem-solving models, partnering and process redesign—to manage environmental, health and safety issues. As discussed by the executives who participated in the study, quality initiatives can help managers reduce operating costs, improve risk assessment, reduce liability exposure and improve efficient allocation of raw materials.

HOW DO I USE IT?

- To determine how quality techniques develop, deploy, measure, and improve environmental health and safety (EH&S) programs in the participating companies;
- To review results achieved by other companies; and
- To help determine the kinds of environmental challenges one's company will face in the next few years.

COST

The cost is $60 for Non-Associates; Associates of The Conference Board receive a substantial discount. (If you are unsure whether your company is an Associate, call Customer Service.)

STRENGTHS AND WEAKNESSES FOR USERS

Experience and expertise from The Conference Board's TQM Center is incorporated into the report. Interviews and viewpoints come from nonpartisan, cross-industry forums on networking and research on leading practices in international EH&S.

The Conference Board is one of the world's leading business membership organizations, with both national and international interests. It is a nonprofit, non-advocacy organization and has over 2,200 member companies. The Conference Board's goal is to enable senior executives from all industries to explore and exchange ideas. It does this through councils, management research, economic information, conferences and seminars and special centers like The Total Quality Management Center.

USER BASE

Not available.

USER SUPPORT

	N/A	Available	Comments
Consultants	x		
Documentation		x	
Training Classes	x		
Telephone Support	x		

VENDOR CONTACT

Wendy Laravuso
Marketing & List Manager
The Conference Board
845 Third Avenue
New York, NY 10022-6601
VOICE   (212) 759-0900

FAX   (212) 980-7014
E-MAIL   laravuso@conference-board.org

TRAINING TECHNOLOGY RESOURCE CENTER

DESCRIPTION

The *Training Technology Resource Center (TTRC)* serves as an electronic point of access to a wide range of workforce development information including innovative workplace practices, occupational skill standards, one-stop career center systems, Job Training Partnership Act issues, school-to-work, and emerging training and learning technologies. Sponsored by the U.S. Department of Labor's Employment and Training Administration, the *TTRC* provides access to this information through an on-line information system via an (800) number and the Internet.

HOW DO I USE IT?

The system is accessed via computer and modem using communications software such as ProComm, Crosstalk, or Smartcom. The system's menu-driven interface allows users to navigate through predefined submenu options or construct their own individualized searches. Any information found on the *TTRC* system can be downloaded as an ASCII file to the user's computer or sent to an e-mail address.

When accessing the *TTRC* using a modem, the communication parameters should be set to 8 data bits, no parity, and 1 stop bit (8-N-1). The terminal emulation should be *vt220 (7 bit)* or *vt100/102*. (TTRC modems answer up to 14.4k bps). From the communication software package, dial (202) 219-5941 or (800) 767-0806.

TTRC is also accessible via the Internet as both a telnet session and a World Wide Web (WWW) site. The telnet address is: *ttrc.doleta.gov.* and the URL address is: *http://www.ttrc.doleta.gov.*

COST

Use of the database is free.

STRENGTHS AND WEAKNESSES FOR USERS

The information is easy to access, and the system is easy to use. *TTRC* actively collects descriptions of innovative programs, practices, research, products, and legislation relevant to the employment and training community. Staff maintain strong linkages with organizations, information centers and training institutions at the state and local level in order to stay apprised of new developments and activities. Great effort is applied to obtaining current information and keeping this information updated.

USER BASE

As a federal information center, the *TTRC* is committed to reaching as wide an audience as possible. Target audiences include employment and training organizations, training practitioners, educators, training policy analysts, the research community, and federal, state, and local government offices.

USER SUPPORT

	N/A	Available	Comments
Consultants	x		
Documentation	x		
Training Classes	x		
Telephone Support		x	Telephone support is available through the Center's (800) number.

VENDOR CONTACT

Training Technology Resource Center
Employment and Training Administration
U.S. Department of Labor, N6507
Washington, DC 20210
Attention: Brian F. Shea, Project Director
VOICE   (202) 219-5600
                    (800) 488-0901
FAX   (202) 219-4858
E-MAIL   ttrc@doleta.gov

WAGE AND FRINGE BENEFIT SURVEY

DESCRIPTION

How much do employees earn in the tooling and machining industry? With this annual survey, managers can compare wage rates for specific jobs with other firms on the regional and national levels. The survey also helps to construct a competitive fringe benefit program by outlining the types and costs of benefits offered by other NTMA members. Furthermore, the report offers competitive advantages; managers can use wage data from other regions in order to make competitive bids. The report gives hourly wage rates and average wages.

HOW DO I USE IT?

Wage information is organized by job title. All major metalworking jobs are covered in the report. The report also describes averages for benefits such as sick days and insurance, as well as various human resource policies.

COST

All NTMA members can receive a free copy of the report. This tool is only available to NTMA members.

STRENGTHS AND WEAKNESSES FOR USERS

The report is the only one of its kind. Since it is based on NTMA membership, it has a broad sample base of participants on which to draw.

USER BASE

NTMA consists of more than 3,000 tooling and machining companies in 56 chapters throughout the U.S. Sixty-five percent of the members have 20 employees or less.

USER SUPPORT

	N/A	Available	Comments
Consultants	x		
Documentation	x		
Training Classes	x		
Telephone Support	x		

VENDOR CONTACT

The National Tooling & Machining Association
9300 Livingston Road
Ft. Washington, MD 20744
VOICE   (301) 248-6200
FAX   (301) 248-7104

WORK PROFILING SYSTEM

DESCRIPTION

Work Profiling System (*WPS*), by Saville & Holdsworth Ltd., is a computerized system that collects, processes, and analyzes relevant job information. *Work Profiling* produces a detailed task description and also specifies the human attributes essential for successful job performance. Specialized reports provide assessments and interview questions for employee selection and promotion; appraisal review forms and compensation models for performance management; and task criticality and context data for reengineering and job design.

HOW DO I USE IT?

Data are gathered using a structured questionnaire which can be administered on computer or in paper and pencil format. Responses are entered into the *Work Profiling Expert System* database for analysis. Companies have the option of installing *WPS* software in-house or sending the data for the Saville & Holdsworth Ltd. bureau to process.

COST

Processing costs are based on the number of questionnaires to be analyzed for a particular job. The first questionnaire is processed by the service bureau for $250; additional questionnaires for the same job are processed at $75. Software may be purchased for in-house analysis, lowering the per questionnaire cost to $40.

STRENGTHS AND WEAKNESSES FOR USERS

Work Profiling provides a solid foundation for linking such organizational functions as selection, training and development, job design, compensation, performance management, and succession planning to a single database. *Work Profiling* is easy-to-learn and can handle virtually any job from entry level to the executive suite.

Any employee can be tested and evaluated against their current position, or they can be compared to the requirements of other positions within the organization to find the best match.

USER BASE

Over 20,000 organizations in 30 countries use Saville & Holdsworth assessment materials. United States users include AT&T, Kodak, and Proctor & Gamble.

USER SUPPORT

	N/A	Available	Comments
Consultants	x		
Documentation		x	
Training Classes		x	
Telephone Support	x		

VENDOR CONTACT

Saville & Holdsworth Ltd.
575 Boylston Street
Boston, MA 02116
VOICE   (800) 899-7451

CHAPTER 3

MARKET AND BUSINESS DEVELOPMENT

ATLANTA ELECTRONIC COMMERCE RESOURCE CENTER

DESCRIPTION

The *Atlanta Electronic Commerce Resource Center (ECRC)* is one of 11 centers established by Congress to help small and medium-sized companies do business more efficiently using Electronic Commerce and Electronic Data Interchange (EC/EDI). Services provided include outreach, education and training, consultation, and technical support. The regional focus of the not-for-profit Atlanta ECRC is Alabama, Florida, Georgia, and South Carolina. Georgia Tech and Clark Atlanta University operate the Atlanta center.

HOW DO I USE IT?

Contact the *Atlanta ECRC* to obtain a schedule of outreach events, courses being offered in the region, or to set up a consultation visit.

COST

The cost of education and training courses is typically $15 per student to cover the cost of materials. Free consultation and technical support is provided, up to as much as 80 hours per client, after which there is fee for service.

STRENGTHS AND WEAKNESSES FOR USERS

Businesses today must use electronic commerce in order to be in business tomorrow. The *Atlanta ECRC* can help companies transition into the new technologies and practices that will become standard procedure in the coming years. With change comes investment in new tools and the learning of new methods and products.

USER BASE

Not Available.

USER SUPPORT

	N/A	Available	Comments
Consultants		x	
Documentation		x	
Training Classes		x	
Telephone Support		x	

VENDOR CONTACT

Atlanta Electronic Commerce Resource Center

Georgia Institute of Technology	Clark Atlanta University
813 Ferst Drive	223 James P. Brawley Drive
Atlanta, GA 30332-0560	Atlanta, GA 30314
VOICE (800) 894-8042	VOICE (404) 880-6939
FAX (404) 894-9342	FAX (404) 941-0406

BizPlan Builder Software

Description
BizPlan Builder contains software and documentation that provides a strategic and business marketing plan on a pre-formatted template. It allows the user to organize ideas, establish direction, and develop a solid foundation for a successful business using existing word processing and spreadsheet software.

How Do I Use It?
Use any DOS, Windows, or Macintosh-based word processor to customize over 90 pages of concise text to fit the requirements of business. To determine financial needs, *BizPlan Builder* offers a full set of financial projections that are pre-formatted in spreadsheet files, featuring formulas that calculate totals, percentages, and ratios. Just fill in the cells with numbers using any popular spreadsheet program.

Cost
BizPlan Builder Software is available to CUED members for $99. Non-members may purchase the software for $129.

Strengths and Weaknesses for Users
The software is useful for quickly developing and publishing an operating plan and budget, a marketing strategy for a new product or service introduction, and a financing presentation for a business venture, a loan, or for refinancing. For maximum utilization of *BizPlan Builder Software*, the user should have some existing knowledge of word processing and spreadsheet software.

User Base
The guide is available through the National Council for Urban Economic Development (CUED), a leading national organization serving economic development practitioners. CUED was founded in 1967 and currently has over 1,500 members.

User Support

	N/A	Available	Comments
Consultants	x		
Documentation		x	
Training Classes	x		
Telephone Support	x		

Vendor Contact
CUED
1730 K Street
Washington, DC 20006
VOICE   (202) 223-4735
FAX   (202) 223-4745

BUSINESS GUIDE TO THE EXPORTING PROCESS

DESCRIPTION

A Business Guide to the Exporting Process is a must-read for any business that is considering entering the global market. This detailed document provides a comprehensive understanding of how to "go global." It walks the reader through a step-by-step process of developing an exporting process. It explains how to assess a company's export potential target market opportunities, enter markets, sell products, and finance the sale. Through a series of worksheets and examples, the reader comes to grips with both the exporting process and his or her business' exporting potential. The guidebook also provides suggestions on where businesses can find export assistance and offers practical advice on pricing, packaging products, and monitoring sales and services.

HOW DO I USE IT?

The 101-page guidebook is organized into the following sections: introduction; why a company should export; the export process—getting started, assessing a company's export potential, researching and targeting market opportunities, options for entering export markets, promotion and advertising, preparing to make a sale, and monitoring and evaluating sales and service. The guidebook also includes a listing of U.S. Department of Commerce District Offices and State International Trade Offices.

COST

A Business Guide to the Exporting Process is available to CUED members for $50 and to nonmembers for $60.

STRENGTHS AND WEAKNESSES FOR USERS

A 1992 study revealed that 90 percent of small businesses surveyed did not export. For many, apprehension and lack of knowledge about the exporting process were the causes. This guidebook offers small businesses the means to integrate exporting strategy into their business operations, thereby potentially greatly expanding their markets.

USER BASE

The guide is available through the National Council for Urban Economic Development (CUED), a leading national organization serving economic development practitioners. CUED was founded in 1967 and currently has over 1,500 members.

USER SUPPORT

	N/A	Available	Comments
Consultants	x		
Documentation	x		
Training Classes	x		
Telephone Support	x		

VENDOR CONTACT
CUED
1730 K Street
Washington, DC 20006
VOICE   (202) 223-4735
FAX   (202) 223-4745

BUSINESS MODERNIZATION TOOLS

DESCRIPTION

Business Modernization Tools: The High-Impact Assessment is a comprehensive assessment system developed by the Indiana Business Modernization and Technology Corporation (IBMT). Designed to assist business and economic development organizations in facilitating a proven total business assessment, *Business Modernization Tools* takes a full-circle look at a business rather than focusing on isolated problems (unlike many existing assessment tools). The IBMT systematic approach focuses on a complete assessment of eleven specific Business and Technical Areas of a firm including: the business and its product or service; sales and marketing; manufacturing operations; finance; quality; materials management; product design engineering; personnel; facilities; management information systems; and environmental/safety issues.

A vital component of the IBMT assessment entails an operationally focused financial review called Benchmarking Information and Financial Analysis Report (BI-FAR). It compares a firm to similar-sized companies in the same SIC (Standard Industrial Code) category and concentrates on operational issues such as inventory, gross margin, cost of goods sold, operating costs, net income, and cash flow. This helps the assessor to prepare and focus on the appropriate questions to ask while conducting the complete assessment.

HOW DO I USE IT?

The assessor holds a one-hour pre-assessment meeting with top management to explain the assessment process and learn about the firm. Financial information is gathered and entered into software for a BI-FAR. The assessor then spends six to eight hours on-site conducting interviews and collecting assessment data. Another 12 hours are spent off-site analyzing the information gathered, identifying performance issues, preparing recommendations, and writing a final report. The assessor goes to the firm to present and review findings and engage key personnel in improvement planning. At this two-to-three hour meeting, an action plan is developed focusing on three or four priority improvement needs. The assessment process includes a phase for action plan implementation with the assessor or others providing encouragement and resources for changes at the firm. The assessor monitors progress at the firm through ongoing financial benchmarking analysis.

COST

Indiana BMT Corporation charges interested organizations $45,000 for two-and-a-half days of on-site training for up to 25 people and provides assessment tools and documents for up to five people. The fee also covers licensing and updates for the tool. Travel expenses for on-site training are additional.

STRENGTHS AND WEAKNESSES FOR USERS

The program is designed to allow assessors to take a comprehensive look at the company in an effective and efficient manner with minimal time demands (a total of 24 person-hours are required). A complete training package is provided with on-site training by an IBMT facilitator. BI-FAR is unique to the assessment system and yields a total financial picture of the business that identifies areas of opportunities for improvement within the company.

USER BASE

The tool became available in 1991 and, as of June 1994, has been used 190 times.

USER SUPPORT

	N/A	Available	Comments
Consultants		x	BMT facilitators train and support.
Documentation		x	BI-FAR aids users.
Training Classes		x	Includes:
			• introductory video;
			• two-and-a-half days on-site training support;
			• complete user's guide + software; and
			• "interactive training."
Telephone Support		x	Business Tools Support at (800) 877-5182.

VENDOR CONTACT

Business Modernization Tools
c/o Corporate Creations
122 South Park Boulevard
Greenwood, IN 46143
VOICE   (317) 889-9680
FAX   (317) 889-2181

CHECKLIST FOR EVALUATING NEW IDEAS AND VENTURES

- THE BUSINESS PLAN: A STATE-OF-THE-ART GUIDE
- THE MARKETING PLAN: STEP-BY-STEP

DESCRIPTION

Checklist for Evaluating New Ideas and Ventures provides manufacturers and entrepreneurs with a method to quickly assess a new product or venture idea against key factors for success. Four primary areas are assessed: 1) technology compared to others; 2) market opportunity; 3) economic feasibility; and 4) management factors. Success factors are utilized for seed and venture capital funding. *Business Plan* and *Market Plan* publications are step-by-step workbooks developed for manufacturing start-up ventures with a new product.

How Do I Use It?

The *Checklist, Business Plan*, and *Market Plan* are printed material specifically designed for first-time users. The publications are step-by-step guides for people who need to be thorough but who want to focus the task quickly. They are not "boilerplate," however, as they require critical thinking skills.

Cost

Checklist for Evaluating New Ideas and Ventures costs $50. *Business Plan: A State-of-the-Art Guide* costs $30 plus $3 shipping and handling. *Marketing Plan: Step-by-Step* costs $30 plus $3 shipping and handling.

Strengths and Weaknesses for Users

This tool offers cost-effective, relatively quick ways to assess the market and economic viability of a new product or venture. All step-by-step processes are prepared for people who have not previously been through the commercialization process. *Checklist* is applicable for most new ventures and products, but not all. Specialized industry or product knowledge may be required for proper evaluation and assessment. *Checklist, Market Plan*, and *Business Plan* workbooks require critical thinking skills by user and realistic self-assessment.

User Base

The *Business Plan: A State-of-the-Art Guide* has sold approximately 51,000 copies since 1988. The *Marketing Plan: Step-by-Step* has sold approximately 22,000 copies since 1992. *Evaluation Checklist* has sold approximately 650 copies since 1991.

User Support

	N/A	Available	Comments
Consultants	x		
Documentation	x		
Training Classes	x		
Telephone Support	x		

Vendor Contact

Center for Innovation & Business Development
100 Harrington Hall, University of North Dakota
P.O. Box 8372
Grand Forks, ND 58202-8372
VOICE   (701) 777-3132
FAX   (701) 777-2339
E-MAIL   gjovig@vm1.nodak.edu

COMPETITIVE ENHANCEMENT AND DEFENSE DIVERSIFICATION NEEDS ASSESSMENT

DESCRIPTION

Competitive Enhancement and Defense Diversification Needs Assessment is an 11-page survey designed to encourage defense diversification as well as increase the competitiveness of small and medium-sized firms nationwide. Sponsored by the Department of Commerce, Bureau of Export Administration (BXA), the purpose of this program is to provide information on existing federal and state government resources available to assist firms in achieving their growth and development, R&D programs, exporting, financing, training, marketing skills, and more.

HOW DO I USE IT?

Simply request of copy of the voluntary needs assessment survey, fill it out, and return it. BXA will analyze the returned survey and then forward company information to those agencies that can provide the greatest assistance. In this way information regarding government programs can be tailored to fit the specific needs of a company.

COST

This referral service is provided at no cost to firms. Classification as a defense subcontractor is not required to benefit from this program. Moreover, company information will not be shared with other participating companies.

STRENGTHS AND WEAKNESSES FOR USERS

Most firms are unaware of available government programs or services that may assist them in competing in the global marketplace. This program includes the cooperation of more than 50 government agencies, major prime contractors, and industry associations.

BXA has assembled an interagency team of experts that includes representatives from the Departments of Commerce, Defense, Labor and Energy, the Small Business Administration, the Environmental Protection Agency, The Export Import Bank, the Federal Laboratory Consortium, and NASA Regional Technology Transfer Centers. Numerous state and local agencies also are participating.

USER BASE

Not Available.

USER SUPPORT

	N/A	Available	Comments
Consultants	x		
Documentation	x		
Training Classes	x		
Telephone Support	x		

VENDOR CONTACT

U.S. Department of Commerce
Bureau of Export Administration
Room 3878 SAD
Washington, DC 20230
VOICE   (202) 482-4060
FAX   (202) 482-5650
E-MAIL   bbotwin@doc.gov

FACTS AND FIGURES OF THE U.S. PLASTICS INDUSTRY 1994

DESCRIPTION

This book offers comprehensive and current information about the plastics industry. Published every autumn, the book highlights production, sales, markets, end uses, and growth rates for major resins. It also includes statistical information on plastics machinery, reinforced plastics shipments, vinyl siding, soffit shipments, and financial data.

HOW DO I USE IT?

The book can be browsed for an overview of the industry, or it can be used to concentrate on sector-specific information.

COST

Quantity 1-2: members of the Society of the Plastics, $95 each; non-members, $190.
Quantity 3-plus: members, $76; non-members; $152.

STRENGTHS AND WEAKNESSES FOR USERS

The book is updated every year, so data is very current. The book provides in-depth data not only about the industry in general but also about industry segments.

USER BASE

Not Available.

USER SUPPORT

	N/A	Available	Comments
Consultants	x		
Documentation		x	
Training Classes	x		
Telephone Support		x	

Vendor Contact

The Society of the Plastics Industry, Inc.
1275 K Street, N.W., #400
Washington, DC 20005-4006
VOICE   (202) 371-5257

Forecast Pro

Description

Forecast Pro, a product of Business Forecast Systems, is a business software that performs statistical forecasting of time series data. It was designed for professionals in sales, marketing, finance, and manufacturing to forecast sales, revenues, expenses, energy use, etc. *Forecast Pro* accepts data in a variety of spreadsheet formats. *Forecast Pro* includes four basic methodologies—moving average, exponential smoothing, Box-Jenkins, and dynamic regression—and selects the most appropriate method for the data entered. It also creates and prints graphs of data and forecasts. It allows someone who is not an expert in statistics or forecasting to produce highly accurate forecasts quickly and easily.

How Do I Use It?

The standard edition of *Forecast Pro* is available in both DOS and Windows versions. *Forecast Pro* requires a DOS compatible computer with two megabytes free on the hard disk and two megabytes of RAM. *Forecast Pro* for Windows also requires Microsoft Windows 3.1, NT, or OS/2 2.1. A math coprocessor and a mouse or trackball are highly recommended.

Forecast Pro uses a simple menu structure and tool bar. The user can import and export data from virtually any source, including Lotus, Excel, ASCII files, and DDE links. The user can put a single time series in row or column format or define one's own, but the user must specify the range within the spreadsheet before importing.

Cost

Forecast Pro (Windows or DOS) is $595. *Forecast Pro* XE (Windows only) for more advanced forecasting problems is $995. Orders are accepted by phone, fax or mail. There is an unconditional 30-day, money-back guarantee.

Strengths and Weaknesses for Users

Forecast Pro can save time if one does occasional forecasting but lacks a statistical background. It produces accurate forecasts without wasting time struggling with a statistics spreadsheet that is more complicated than one may need.

BYTE Magazine, PC World, and *PC Magazine* all rated *Forecast Pro* highest of the available forecast softwares for accuracy, ease of use, seasonal forecasting, and reports and graphs.

USER BASE

Forecast Pro is a fairly generic product for use by many types of businesses. It does have applications for manufacturers such as forecasting product sales and demand for materials; however, it is not specialized for any particular industry. Companies that use it tend to be larger firms that have forecasting departments.

USER SUPPORT

	N/A	Available	Comments
Consultants	x		
Documentation		x	Complete documentation including tutorial and statistical reference.
Training Classes		x	Business Forecast Systems conducts forecasting seminars in various locations or customized on-site workshops.
Telephone Support		x	Registered *Forecast Pro* owners receive free technical support via telephone, mail and fax.

VENDOR CONTACT

Business Forecast Systems
68 Leonard Street
Belmont, Massachusetts 02178
Attn: Eric Stellwagen, Vice President
VOICE   (617) 484-5050
FAX   (617) 484-9219

GRANT THORNTON LLP

DESCRIPTION

Grant Thornton LLP is one of the nation's largest accounting and management consulting firms, specializing in serving manufacturers and distributors. In addition to providing comprehensive tax, audit, and management consulting services, *Grant Thornton LLP* publishes the annual *Grant Thornton Survey of American Manufacturers and Manufacturing Issues*, a quarterly newsletter devoted to these industries. Through its national and international presence, Grant Thornton professionals provide broad-based business advice as well as targeted technical assistance.

HOW DO I USE IT?

To receive further information or to be added to the *Manufacturing Issues* mailing list, contact the closest Grant Thornton office.

COST

Newsletters and brochures are free. Services are priced on an hourly or project basis.

STRENGTHS AND WEAKNESSES FOR USERS

Grant Thornton LLP delivers major international firm resources combined with local firm attention and service. Partners and managers are actively involved with each client and serve as value-added business advisers.

USER BASE

It operates 500 offices including 85 countries worldwide and 48 U.S. cities. Tax and audit services are provided to middle-market manufacturers/distributors. Management consulting is provided to both mid-sized and large manufacturers and distributors.

USER SUPPORT

	N/A	Available	Comments
Consultants	x		
Documentation	x		
Training Classes		x	
Telephone Support	x		

VENDOR CONTACT

Mr. Ronald Baum, Managing Partner
Grant Thornton LLP - Atlanta Office
2300 North Tower
235 Peachtree Street, N.E.
Atlanta, GA 30329
VOICE   (404) 330-2000
FAX   (404) 330-2047

GUERRILLA ADVERTISING: COST-EFFECTIVE TACTICS FOR SMALL BUSINESS SUCCESS

DESCRIPTION

This book focuses Jay Conrad Levinson's famous guerrilla marketing techniques on advertising. Advertising is the most elusive and expensive part of any marketing campaign. Step-by-step chapters cover the key components of an advertising project: advertising strategy, effective ads and copy, advertising effectiveness, audience focus, budgeting, and medium management.

How Do I Use It?

This book provides nuts-and-bolts steps of cost-effective advertising for small businesses. Each chapter covers a particular facet of the advertising campaign.

Cost

The book costs $11.95.

Strengths and Weaknesses for Users

The major strength of this book is also its major weakness. It provides focused instructions on mounting an advertising campaign, but it does not place advertising in its role as only part of an entire marketing campaign. However, other publications in the *Guerilla Marketing* series can address this limitation.

User Base

Not Available.

User Support

	N/A	Available	Comments
Consultants	x		
Documentation		x	
Training Classes	x		
Telephone Support	x		

Vendor Contact

Houghton Mifflin Company
215 Park Avenue South
New York, NY 10003
VOICE   (800) 225-3362
FAX   (212) 420-5850

Guerrilla Marketing Excellence: The Fifty Golden Rules for Small-Business Success

Description

Jay Conrad Levinson, guerrilla marketing guru, has created 50 basic truths that can make or break small and medium-sized companies. The newest addition to the guerrilla marketing books lists general lessons to follow in order to avoid marketing pitfalls while increasing sales.

How Do I Use It?

The book divides the 50 rules into functional areas: guiding thinking, guiding effectiveness, guiding marketing materials, guiding campaigns. Each area consists of several rules, followed by explanations of the rules.

Cost

The book costs $9.95.

Strengths and Weaknesses for Users

The book says that the advice "appears in the guise of basic home truths, many of which are already part of your own good common sense." The entire thrust of the book is much more abstract than the other guerrilla books.

User Base

Not Available.

User Support

	N/A	Available	Comments
Consultants	x		
Documentation		x	
Training Classes	x		
Telephone Support	x		

Vendor Contact

Houghton Mifflin Company
215 Park Avenue South
New York, NY 10003
VOICE   (800) 225-3362
FAX   (212) 420-5850

The Guerrilla Marketing Handbook

Description

This handbook explains how small and medium-sized companies can get the maximum marketing bang for their buck. It stresses high impact techniques at minimal costs. The book is divided into three sections: Tactics and Strategies; Creating a Plan That Works; Covering the Nuts and Bolts of a Marketing Plan; and The Guerrilla Marketing Arsenal, covering marketing techniques; and the Appendix, a list of resources.

How Do I Use It?

The handbook guides readers through the steps necessary for a successful marketing campaign. Users simply follow the manual.

Cost

The book costs $16.95.

STRENGTHS AND WEAKNESSES FOR USERS

The book is not theoretical; it offers concrete plans that lead to concrete actions. The book's plans are very realistic in terms acknowledging the costs involved in such campaigns and the finite amount of funds available for such pursuits.

USER BASE

Not Available.

USER SUPPORT

	N/A	Available	Comments
Consultants	x		
Documentation		x	
Training Classes	x		
Telephone Support	x		

VENDOR CONTACT

Houghton Mifflin Company
215 Park Avenue South
New York, NY 10003
VOICE   (800) 225-3362
FAX   (212) 420-5850

GUERRILLA MARKETING ON-LINE

DESCRIPTION

Authored by Jay Conrad Levinson and Charles Rubin, this book explains how to use the power of the Internet to market products. The Internet is the international computer network that allows for inexpensive, yet comprehensive marketing exposure. The book describes the on-line marketplace, explains strategies for using the new technology, and gives detailed advice on how to manage the marketing campaign. Special emphasis is on how this new technology differs as a marketing tool from the standard marketing delivery channels.

HOW DO I USE IT?

The book is divided into easily understood chapters that address different needs. Although the first sections of the book give necessary information about the Internet, the last section offers concrete steps on using the technology.

COST

The book costs $12.95.

STRENGTHS AND WEAKNESSES FOR USERS

Unlike some of the guerrilla marketing books, this book contains much more descriptive than prescriptive instructions. The dynamic, technically evolving nature of the Internet necessitates this approach.

USER BASE

Not Available.

USER SUPPORT

	N/A	Available	Comments
Consultants	x		
Documentation		x	
Training Classes	x		
Telephone Support	x		

VENDOR CONTACT

Houghton Mifflin Company
215 Park Avenue South
New York, NY 10003
VOICE   (800) 225-3362
FAX   (212) 420-5850

IBEX—THE INTERNATIONAL BUSINESS EXCHANGE

DESCRIPTION

IBEX is an electronic, interactive system that facilitates finding, qualifying, and negotiating directly with prospective business partners, both foreign and domestic. It addresses all the details of conducting a business transaction: producing a purchase order, attaching a sales contract, procuring credit references, arranging distribution, etc.

HOW DO I USE IT?

IBEX is easily installed on any personal computer running Windows with a modem. After installation, the user enters a concise company profile and then makes an offer or request for a product, service, support service, or investment opportunity. One can electronically attach any pertinent information, such as price lists, brochures, or specs. This information is sent via e-mail to a server, which will automatically find suitable matches among the worldwide *IBEX* subscription base. An e-mail and/or fax message will alert the user that a match has been found. Negotiation, clarification and mutual qualification continue until a deal is struck.

COST

The initial subscription fee is $250, which includes the actual *IBEX* software as well as AT&T Access Plus, a complete e-mail system. Monthly charges are based entirely upon customer usage. One pays a fee for each function, which are for the most part in the single digits.

STRENGTHS AND WEAKNESSES FOR USERS

There are several key advantages to this program, including:

- **Quality Control.** All subscribers fill out profiles containing bank and trade references. All offers are anonymous, giving each party an opportunity to question prospective partners and offers prior to any commitment. On-line credit checks are available.
- **Confidentiality.** The user controls security at every stage. Negotiations are only accessible to the parties involved; profiles are released when and to whom the subscriber determines.
- **Ease of Use.** *IBEX* Windows-based software makes entering and responding to offers or requesting commercial information as easy as "point and click."
- **Cost.** Transactions on *IBEX* cost only a fraction of the average cost of finding and negotiating with a partner via conventional means.
- **Speed.** *IBEX* automatically matches the querent with offers meeting the business needs one designates, reducing the time one would otherwise spend searching for, screening and negotiating with business partners who may or may not be viable.

USER BASE

IBEX is a global system. One can use it to find business partners in one's own city or in another country.

USER SUPPORT

	N/A	Available	Comments
Consultants		x	
Documentation		x	
Training Classes		x	
Telephone Support		x	

VENDOR CONTACT

IBEX
U.S. Chamber of Commerce
1615 H Street, N.W. 6th Floor
Washington, DC 20062-2000
VOICE (800) 537-IBEX
In District of Columbia, call (202) 463-5665

LITERATURE CATALOGUE 1995-1996— THE SOCIETY OF THE PLASTICS INDUSTRY, INC.

DESCRIPTION

See listing in Human Resources section, page 38.

MANUFACTURING ASSISTANCE PROGRAM NEEDS ASSESSMENT GUIDE

DESCRIPTION

The *Manufacturing Assistance Program Needs Assessment Guide* describes approaches used and recommended by assistance program staff to assess manufacturers' needs. The guide consists of two volumes: *Volume 1: Regional Needs Assessment Approaches* and *Volume 2: Firm-Level Needs Assessment Approaches.*

HOW DO I USE IT?

These volumes can be used together or as stand-alone documents. Each volume presents a selection of specific approaches for conducting manufacturing needs assessments. The discussion of each approach includes: a description, a statement of its use and intentions, one or more case examples showing how the approach has been used by actual manufacturing assistance programs, a summary of its strengths and weaknesses, and sources for more information.

COST

The cost is $12 for each single-volume copy or $20 for the two-volume set. Bulk discounts are available. Copies can be ordered by calling The Aspen Institute's Publications Office at (410) 820-5326.

STRENGTHS AND WEAKNESSES FOR USERS

In using the material in these volumes, please note the following: 1) This material is not intended to represent "best practices;" 2) Assessment tools and methods are continually evolving; 3) The inclusion of particular case examples, references and contacts are not intended to be endorsements; and 4) There is no single "right" approach.

USER BASE

Volume 1 was written primarily for directors of technical and management assistance programs serving private industry within a region to help them during program start-up. *Volume 2* was written primarily for directors and staff of technical and management assistance programs who are conducting ongoing work with a targeted set of firms. The guide also can be used as a resource by manufacturing assistance program planners and marketing staff, researchers of industrial policy and technology diffusion, people involved in economic development activities serving business, private sector management consultants, and industry and technology policymakers.

USER SUPPORT

	N/A	Available	Comments
Consultants	x		
Documentation		x	Sources for more information about each approach are provided in the text.
Training Classes	x		
Telephone Support	x		

VENDOR CONTACT

Rural Economic Policy Program
The Aspen Institute
1333 New Hampshire Avenue, NW
Suite 1070
Washington, DC 20036
VOICE (202) 736-5804
FAX (202) 467-0790

MARKETING ADVISORS ™ (MARKET ENGINEERING TOOLS)

OVERALL DESCRIPTION

Market Engineering Tools can help even those without formal marketing backgrounds to plan and implement successful marketing efforts. They have proven successful in a wide range of applications, incorporating the best marketing practices of industry. These innovative tools are especially effective in high-tech environments.

Managers can utilize any of the six ADVISORS to accomplish results in the following areas:

- **Team Focus** *(The TEAM ADVISOR)*—Where the team wants to go (strategic directions), and how it will get there (strategic decisions);
- **Market Definitions** *(The MARKETS ADVISOR)*—Applications, markets, customers, and market research to confirm and extend team knowledge;
- **Product Value** *(The PRODUCTS ADVISOR)*—Customers, needs, benefits, product differentiation, desired perceptions, mission, name, and product identity;

- **Goals, Strategies, and Plans** *(The ACTIONS ADVISOR)*—Engineering of marketing actions by setting goals, selecting viable strategies to meet the goals, and planning implementation of the strategies;
- **Communications** *(The COMMUNICATIONS ADVISOR)*—Engineering of messages of value into marketing communications to assure effective information transfer and perception management; and
- **Marketing Events** *(The TRADE-SHOW ADVISOR)*—Planning and preparation for all activities necessary to achieve organizational goals through marketing events.

In summary, the MARKETING ADVISORS are unique, self-consistent team processes that implement the science of marketing as a set of licensable, transferable tools for effective marketing *and* technology transfer. Moreover, new tools may be assembled by combining tool elements appropriate for specific situations.

STRENGTHS AND WEAKNESSES FOR USERS

The MARKETING ADVISORS™ are complete tools developed in the fashion of a software product. They come with an ADVISOR'S manual, ADVISOR'S training, complete background material, and support from Market Engineering International.

The MARKETING ADVISORS are designed for use by specialists working with clients who have little practical experience in marketing, including young companies, entrepreneurs, R&D labs, engineering firms, and defense contractors. If these demanding clients can be served, it is assumed that other clients will also be satisfied.

The ADVISORS work with the strengths of technical professionals and business people. Hypothesis-raising can create confrontational interactions, so few hypotheses are raised. Instead, questions are asked that rapidly achieve desired goals through the natural tendency to brainstorm to solutions. Results are achieved without turning the brainstorming team into marketers.

Market Engineering methods are based upon industry best practices but are reduced to the essentials necessary to accomplish desired results. When used properly, MARKETING ADVISORS deliver the full benefits of marketing, including higher funding and revenues, lower costs, improved customer relationships, stronger competitive advantage, and a durable, positive image.

COST

Single end-user license fees and training costs are shown in the table. License are discounted for multiple licenses by one user and for licenses for more than one MARKETING ADVISOR. Licenses are always awarded to an organization, not to an individual person.

Consultants pay no license fee but do pay for training as well as submitting a royalty on revenues generated from use.

Marketing Advisor™	License Fee	Training Time	Training Costs*
The TEAM ADVISOR	$8,000	8 days	$8,000
The MARKETS ADVISOR	6,000	6 days	6,000
The PRODUCTS ADVISOR	8,000	7 days	7,000
The ACTIONS ADVISOR	6,000	6 days	6,000
The COMMUNICATIONS ADVISOR	6,000	7 days	7,000
The TRADE-SHOW ADVISOR	6,000	6 days	6,000

Travel expenses are not included.

USER BASE

MARKETING ADVISORS have been used in the service of high-technology companies of all sizes, research departments of major companies, government labs, defense contractors, SBIR companies, universities, and independent research organizations.

USER SUPPORT

	N/A	Available	Comments
Consultants		x	
Documentation		x	
Training Classes		x	
Telephone Support		x	

VENDOR CONTACT

Dr. Gary M. Lundquist, President
Market Engineering International, Inc.
12006 N. Antelope Trail
Parker, CO 80134
VOICE   (303) 840-9929
FAX   (303) 841-6636

MARKET SCOUT

DESCRIPTION

Market Scout is a unique, quick-turnaround facilitating process that provides a snapshot marketing report that can identify markets for current products and new product options. This process is used when a company wishes to examine market and product diversification options given its current equipment, machinery, and personnel capabilities. The *Market Scout* process is applicable to companies utilizing metalcutting, forming, joining, bending, welding, and assembling equipment. Company data is used to create custom Market Scout Market Selection Guides.

HOW DO I USE IT?

Market Scout is provided through the Industrial Technology Institute. If a manufacturer fits the *Market Scout* requirements, data is collected on: 1) machinery and equipment; 2) personnel; and 3) marketing issues via questionnaires. Subsequently, a *Market Scout* report is created.

COST

- Market Scout Market Selection Guides: Generic Industry Report—$450; Custom Company Report—$2,500
- Market Scout Customer Identification Guides (six industries analyzed and purchasing leads identified): Vol. 1 (off-shelf available)—$900
- Add-on Modules for Market Selection Guides: Competitive Analysis, Forecasting, Purchasing Leads—$3,000-plus (each)

Other industry market analyses can be prepared with cost relative to effort.

STRENGTHS AND WEAKNESSES FOR USERS

This unique, quantitative system matches actual capabilities with emerging opportunities. Add-on Modules provide the capacity to add customized tactics/action plans.

USER BASE

This process is utilized by market analysts, and its reports are utilized by managers and decisionmakers.

USER SUPPORT

	N/A	Available	Comments
Consultants	x		
Documentation	x		
Training Classes	x		
Telephone Support		x	

VENDOR CONTACT

Industrial Technology Institute
2901 Hubbard Road
Ann Arbor, MI 48105
VOICE   (313) 769-4000

Attn: Mr. Aayush Asthana, Project Manager
VOICE   (313) 769-4652
FAX   (313) 769-4064
E-MAIL   aa@iti.org

NEWPROD

DESCRIPTION

NewProd, a service of The Adept Group, is based on an advanced statistical model that assesses the strengths and weaknesses of a potential new product and predicts its likelihood of success. The model enables users to compare their new product against a large database of earlier new product launches, of which half succeeded and half failed. The model can be used to screen new product ideas or to determine which characteristics of a new product would be most advantageous to change. Numerous independent studies have validated the accuracy of the model.

HOW DO I USE IT?

NewProd can be used by completing one or more surveys. The survey asks a total of 30 questions. The questions reflect on resources, distribution, degree of innovativeness, market attractiveness, competition, technology, price, production, management, and customers. Surveys are returned to The Adept Group via fax, mail, or overnight service. Analysis is conducted and summary reports are returned within 48 hours. Up to one hour of consulting is given to supplement all analysis reports.

COST

The base fee for a single analysis by a single evaluator is $300. Each additional evaluation is $50. A site license and training in the model and its application ranges between $25,000 and $50,000, depending upon company size.

STRENGTHS AND WEAKNESSES FOR USERS

The regression models employed are impressive and have been finely tuned to ensure statistical validity and reliability. The full-fledged product will be cost-prohibitive for many, but a single analysis is a much less costly option.

USER BASE

NewProd is used around the world by companies active in developing and launching new products. Well-known users include such firms as E.I. Dupont, S.C. Johnson, Polaroid, Dow, Eastman Chemical, Pitney Bowes, Eaton, and ProCon Products.

USER SUPPORT

	N/A	Available	Comments
Consultants		x	
Documentation		x	
Training Classes		x	Customized on-site classes.
Telephone Support		x	

VENDOR CONTACT

Mr. Paul O'Connor
Managing Director
The Adept Group, Ltd.

#110 Southpoint Blvd.
Suite 230
Jacksonville, FL 32216
VOICE   (904) 296-3256
FAX   (904) 296-3149

OUTLINE FOR A BUSINESS PLAN

DESCRIPTION

This generalized approach to writing a business plan, along with the careful analysis required, can help entrepreneurs determine the feasibility of financing a new company, anticipate the questions potential investors may ask, and develop a more detailed operating plan.

HOW DO I USE IT?

Outline for a Business Plan instructs the user on how to create a business plan outline with the following series of steps: executive summary; market analysis; company description; marketing and sales activities; products and services; operations; management and ownership; funds required and their uses; financial data; and appendices or exhibits. Additionally, the 16-page reference guide describes uses of a business plan, steps in preparing a business plan, administrative considerations, and information for entrepreneurs.

COST

The reference guide is free of charge.

STRENGTHS AND WEAKNESSES FOR USERS

The guide serves as a good quick and simple reference for business plan outlines and should be taken as such. It is not a particularly detailed guide. The fact that the guide is free of charge is a plus.

USER BASE

The reference guide has been employed by numerous entrepreneurs wishing to develop a business plan. Ernst & Young LLP's National Entrepreneurial Services create value with capabilities through financing assistance, international expansion, information management, wealth building and retention, and acquisitions and divestitures.

USER SUPPORT

	N/A	Available	Comments
Consultants		x	
Documentation		x	
Training Classes		x	
Telephone Support		x	

Vendor Contact
    Ernst & Young LLP
    National Entrepreneurial Services
    2001 Ross Avenue, Suite 2800
    Dallas, TX 75201
    VOICE   (214) 979-1700
    FAX   (214) 979-2333

PAINT AND COATINGS "2000": REVIEW AND FORECAST

DESCRIPTION

This new report provides an analysis of economic trends and their impact on coatings; a quantitative review and projections of technological and regulatory changes in the paint and coatings industry; and projections of industry growth by market segments to the year 2000.

HOW DO I USE IT?

The report is extensively formatted with graphs and charts for easy reading and covers key factors that impact the U.S. market for coatings products. Profiled markets include: architectural coatings, product coatings (OEM) and special purpose coatings. The *Paint and Coatings "2000": Review and Forecast* is an excellent planning and decision-making tool for marketers of paint and coatings, paint and coatings raw materials, and application equipment.

COST

For members, the report costs $465 for the first copy; $280 each additional copy. For non-members, the price is $1,100 per copy.

STRENGTHS AND WEAKNESSES FOR USERS

The National Paint and Coatings Association's management information committee worked with Kline & Company, a leading consulting firm, and a select group of industry experts to ensure that readers receive the most credible and useful information possible.

USER BASE

NPCA is a voluntary, nonprofit trade association representing some 500 paint and coatings manufacturers, raw materials suppliers, and distributors. Collectively, NPCA's membership produces approximately 75 percent of the total dollar-volume of paints and industrial coatings sold in the United States.

USER SUPPORT

	N/A	Available	Comments
Consultants	x		
Documentation	x		

	N/A	Available	Comments
Training Classes	x		
Telephone Support		x	

VENDOR CONTACT

National Paint and Coatings Association
1500 Rhode Island Avenue, NW
Washington, DC 20005
VOICE (202) 462-6272
FAX (202) 462-8549

QUARTERLY CUSTOMER MARKET AND BUSINESS FORECAST REPORTS

DESCRIPTION

These quarterly reports provide industry-specific information about projected sales of tool and die products and the projected economic condition of the industries that purchase tool and die products.

The *Customer Market Forecast Report* shows projected shipments in the industries with the largest consumption of machinist products and services: motor vehicles and parts; household appliances; construction, oil, and mining equipment; electronic components; and aircraft, space vehicles, and missiles.

The *Business Forecast Report* describes projected sales of the following machinists product segments: tools, dies, and fixtures; precision machining; aerospace machining and fabrication; molds; and special machines.

HOW DO I USE IT?

Both reports contain written commentary as well as graphs and tables to illustrate the mechanisms affecting the tool and die industry.

COST

The reports are distributed free to NTMA members. Non-members may receive free single copies upon request.

STRENGTHS AND WEAKNESSES FOR USERS

The reports provide a concise description of the macroeconomic environment that affects machine shops on a daily basis. Although this information can be uncovered elsewhere, gathering such focused information would require extensive research on the part of a shop manager.

USER BASE

NTMA consists of more than 3,000 tooling and machining companies in 56 chapters throughout the U.S. Sixty-five percent of the members have 20 employees or less.

USER SUPPORT

	N/A	Available	Comments
Consultants	x		
Documentation	x		
Training Classes	x		
Telephone Support	x		

VENDOR CONTACT

The National Tooling & Machining Association
9300 Livingston Road
Ft. Washington, MD 20744
VOICE (301) 248-6200
FAX (301) 248-7104

STAGE-GATE PROCESS

DESCRIPTION

The *Stage-Gate Process* is a systematic approach to improve success rates for new products and reduce their time to market. The process, championed by Dr. Robert Cooper of McMaster University, divides innovation into stages from idea conception to commercialization. Each stage consists of cross functional, concurrent team activities. Successive sages address issues in more depth. Gates, or decision points, follow each Stage. The information obtained in each stage is compared to established criteria. "Go" decisions commit resources for the next stage. Criteria become more demanding as the project advances.

HOW DO I USE IT?

The *Stage-Gate Process* becomes a part of a new product development efforts. It is a simple concept, although implementation is complex. Each company has its own culture and needs, and a process is designed around these. A detailed document is prepared that outlines how the process will be operated in the company. Training is an essential part of implementing the process. Everyone in the organization, particularly top management, must be on board for the process to obtain the expected benefits.

COST

There is no cost for the basic model. Dr. Cooper has written many articles and books describing the process and the basis for its success. The difficulty comes in understanding the problems of operating the system, and what safeguards are needed to avoid operational problems after the system is in place. An experienced facilitator can move the company in the right direction with regard to the basic model, the criteria, and decision-making at each gate, and training.

STRENGTHS AND WEAKNESSES FOR USERS

The *Stage-Gate Process* is a road map to new products. If properly implemented, it results in an improved success rate for new product introductions. It is visible to everyone in the company, so all can feel that they have a chance to test their ideas. The requirements are clear, so there are no surprises because failures are caught early. The system requires team effort, which builds confidence in the participants. It provides a continuous measure of where the total new product effort stands at any time. It is also a customer-oriented and market-driven process which helps ensure the ultimate success of the project.

The weaknesses in the process are that it requires discipline and continuous training, as well as process improvements when problems are recognized. High-level employees are required to be participants, which is sometimes difficult for busy executives.

USER BASE

Not available.

USER SUPPORT

	N/A	Available	Comments
Consultants		x	
Documentation	x		
Training Classes	x		
Telephone Support	x		

VENDOR CONTACT

Dr. Larry Plonsker
President
Chemical Network Associates, Inc.
1819 Applewood Road
Baton Rouge, LA 70808
VOICE   (504) 769-1783
FAX   (504) 769-1792
E-MAIL   cxn11a@prodigy.com

TEXAS-ONE

DESCRIPTION

TEXAS-ONE, a product of the Texas Department of Commerce, offers an electronic information system with a menu of options to state, national, and global information services relevant to small business. Its purpose is to improve business competitiveness through productive use of the

Internet. Toward that end, *TEXAS-ONE* collaborates with Texas state government, education, and private organizations that offer public information delivery services.

TEXAS-ONE features a number of sub-menus. A "General Information" area offers training and consulting directories, a "What's New" section, Internet navigation tools and resources for developers, and general information about the *TEXAS-ONE* project. A "Business Information Collection" area offers a wide range of business resources organized by category and featuring key word search capability. An area called "The Texas Marketplace" focuses on market opportunities including procurement leads, international trade leads, business directories, and buyer/seller marketing services.

How Do I Use It?

TEXAS-ONE may accessed through the World Wide Web (WWW) with the following URL: *http://www.texas-one.org*. One may also gopher to the following address: *gopher.texas-one.org*. TEXAS-ONE staff are also working with Internet access providers to have *TEXAS-ONE* placed on their main menus.

Cost

The main cost is associated with the regular charges levied by one's Internet Service Provider. Rates vary depending on one's location and level of service chosen. *TEXAS-ONE* points to a few commercial services that charge a fee, but the majority of the information is free.

Strengths and Weaknesses for Users

TEXAS-ONE is unique because it offers high-quality data based on customer needs, "help" documentation that is easily understood, easy searching and navigation, a standard look and feel to thousands of different information resource sites, and continual improvements to the system. Furthermore, *TEXAS-ONE* is provided as a free service.

User Base

Key participants in the *TEXAS-ONE* Project include: Texas Department of Commerce; Texas Department of Information Resources; University of Texas at El Paso; Mid-Continent Technology Transfer Center at Texas A&M University; Texas Small Business Development Centers; Microelectronics and Computer Technology Corporation; Department of Defense-funded Electronic Commerce Resource Centers; Advanced Research Projects Agency; National Institute of Standards and Technology; and Texas Innovation Network.

User Support

	N/A	Available	Comments
Consultants	x		
Documentation	x		
Training Classes	x		
Telephone Support		x	

VENDOR CONTACT

Texas Department of Commerce
Office of Advanced Technology
P.O. Box 12728
Austin, TX 78711
VOICE   (800) 888-0511 or
             (512) 936-0081
FAX   (512) 936-0440
E-MAIL   comment@texas-one.org
URL   http://www.texas-one.org

TRADE INFORMATION CENTER

DESCRIPTION

The *Trade Information Center* is a comprehensive resource for information on all federal government export assistance programs. The Center is operated by the U.S. Department of Commerce for the 19 federal agencies comprising the Trade Promotion Coordinating Committee (TPCC). Services provided include referral information on market research sources, domestic and international trade events, export financing, export licenses and documentation, and other government assistance programs. International Trade Specialists at the Center will also provide basic export counseling.

HOW DO I USE IT?

The user can reach an international trade specialist at the Center through a nationwide toll-free number: (800) 872-8723. The Center is open from 8:30 a.m. to 5:30 p.m., Monday through Friday, Eastern Time. A fax-on-demand document retrieval system is available 24 hours a day.

COST

There is no charge for the Center's services.

STRENGTHS AND WEAKNESSES FOR USERS

The Center is a valuable source of information on exporting U.S. products and services. Questions regarding importing into the U.S. should be directed to the appropriate foreign consulate or trade office. Questions regarding duties on imports should be directed to U.S. Customs.

USER BASE

The Center serves a variety of businesses, both small and large, across the U.S.

USER SUPPORT

	N/A	Available	Comments
Consultants	x		

	N/A	Available	Comments
Documentation		x	The Center publishes *Export Programs: A Business Directory of Government Services*.
Training Classes	x		
Telephone Support		x	

VENDOR CONTACT

The Trade Information Center
U.S. Department of Commerce
International Trade Administration
Room HCHB 7424
Washington, DC 20230
VOICE & FAX-ON-DEMAND   (800) USA-TRADE
TDD   (800) 833-8723

WINNING AND COMMERCIALIZING SBIR

(THE SBIR/STTR OUTREACH PROGRAM ELECTRONIC MANUAL)

DESCRIPTION

This manual was prepared by Foresight Science and Technology for a NSF/DoD-funded program to train state and local economic development officials. The manual covers topics such as marketing, locating relevant technical and market information, commercialization, partnering, business plan development, intellectual property, and contract negotiation. An extensive catalog of all major federal R&D activities is provided, together with information on points of contact for general technical marketing, SBIR, and technology transfer. Templates for various tasks are provided as part of the manual.

The manual contains an updated and expanded version of the National Science Foundation's *Small Business Guide to Federal R&D Funding Opportunities* (also written by Foresight Science & Technology). Material from *Foresight's Commercializing Technology* manual has been added, as well as new material. A prototype of the manual was used in a training program for the Boeing Company.

HOW DO I USE IT?

The manual requires a Windows operating system. An ASCII text version for other operating systems is also available. Both versions are available for download from the Foresight server at *http://www.seeport.com* or via ftp to seeport.com. For ftp, the path is SBIR/Manuals. The hypertext file is SBIR.HPL. RTF and TXT versions are also available. Download the HLP file and open it using File Manager. RTF or TXT versions can be opened with a word processor.

Cost

This document was developed under a contract from the National Science Foundation. There is no cost for the document. Duplication and dissemination are encouraged.

Strengths and Weaknesses for Users

For 15 years, Foresight Science and Technology has been providing technical marketing and commercialization to companies, government agencies, universities, and nonprofit organizations. This manual builds on prior documents and has proven useful in numerous training programs.

User Base

This manual has been evaluated as very helpful by participants in the Boeing and the NSF-sponsored State Outreach training programs. It currently is disseminated by SBIR program managers, state officials, and others.

User Support

	N/A	Available	Comments
Consultants	x		
Documentation	x		
Training Classes	x		
Telephone Support		x	

Vendor Contact

Philip Speser, J.D., Ph.D.
Foresight Science and Technology Incorporated
1200 W. Sims Way, Suite 201
Port Townsend, WA 98368
VOICE   (206) 385-9560
E-MAIL   3446234@mci.com

CHAPTER 4

ORGANIZATIONAL REENGINEERING AND REDESIGN

ACHIEVING ENTERPRISE EXCELLENCE

DESCRIPTION

Achieving Enterprise Excellence (AEE) is a comprehensive self-assessment program and management tool designed to determine the current state of a company's enterprise in relation to world-class requirements for excellence. Developed by the National Center for Manufacturing Sciences (NCMS) in Ann Arbor, Michigan, this tool allows organizations to have an in-house, cross-functional team assess and compare existing company practices and policies and benchmark them against a world-class standard. This standard was established by creating a composite of all the requirements of the leading world-class quality standards and programs.

HOW DO I USE IT?

The self-assessment is performed by a team selected from within the company. The team is trained in the use of the assessment materials in a one-day workshop. The three-part *AEE* program consists of: 1) a reference narrative of the requirements for excellence; 2) a self-assessment process to benchmark against these requirements for excellence; and 3) an improvement process.

COST

AEE materials are available from NCMS for $300 each. Training workshops, which include the materials, are provided by NCMS licensees located throughout the country. Workshop fees vary by location but are typically about $500 per person.

STRENGTHS AND WEAKNESSES FOR USERS

The program can be used by companies with any of the following objectives in mind: 1) to develop Total Quality Management (TQM) for the company; 2) to use as a planning tool for both business and operational needs; 3) to use as a framework for a formal continuous improvement program; 4) to use as a supplier development program; 5) to cope with multiple customer quality standards or requirements; or 6) to prepare for compliance documentation or customer site visits.

USER BASE

AEE is the successor to the Achieving Manufacturing Excellence, which has been tested with more than 150 companies.

USER SUPPORT

	N/A	Available	Comments
Consultants	x		
Documentation		x	Licensees are available to consult.
Training Classes		x	Provided by licensees.
Telephone Support		x	

VENDOR CONTACT

National Center for Manufacturing Sciences
3025 Boardwalk

Ann Arbor, MI 48108-3266
Attn: Mike Gnam
VOICE   (313) 995-4971
FAX   (313) 995-1150

ADVANTIG

DESCRIPTION

The *Advanced Manufacturing Technology Implementation Game (ADVANTIG)* is a role-playing simulation of running a manufacturing company. Participants spend a day managing company strategy, making products, developing business and working with suppliers, customers, partners, competitors and unions. A facilitator debriefs lessons learned in organization, communication, decision-making, planning, technology implementation and related facets of operating an industrial business. *ADVANTIG* can be customized for single or multiple-day activities and different company objectives. It is useful for training and education and for company planning. The simulation comes complete with a production landscape and equipment, players' manuals and related materials.

HOW DO I USE IT?

ADVANTIG can be used as a stand-alone training/awareness activity, a practical example for company strategic planning or assessment, or a part of a broader professional development program for students, managers, service-providers and manufacturing employees. One may hire *ADVANTIG* as a service and/or license the simulation and use one's own certified facilitators. *ADVANTIG* can be used as a module in technical or "soft-skill" training programs.

COST

One-day *ADVANTIG* sessions cost $5,000, including materials, preparation/planning and on-site facilitation by two qualified trainers. This session can accommodate 10-18 participants. Multiple concurrent simulations can be offered for larger groups. Corporate licenses with certification training are available for $28,000; licenses for educational institutions are available at lower cost.

STRENGTHS AND WEAKNESSES FOR USERS

ADVANTIG is a powerful action-learning tool for the developing professional or company manager. It is realistic, flexible and demanding. It is also complex and demanding on the facilitator/trainer and requires replenishment of expendable (paper) materials, as well as storage and maintenance of the equipment kit. Corporate leaders from GE, EDS, Michigan Bell and others have enthusiastically supported and repetitively used *ADVANTIG*.

USER SUPPORT

	N/A	Available	Comments
Consultants		x	Available via ITI, Stan Przybylinski (313-769-4517).

	N/A	Available	Comments
Documentation		x	
Training Classes		x	Certification training with license purchase.
Telephone Support		x	Telephone support available for questions.

VENDOR CONTACT

Stan Przybylinski
ITI
P.O. Box 1485
Ann Arbor, MI 48106
VOICE   (313) 769-4517
E-MAIL   smp@iti.org

BENCHMARKING: THE SEARCH FOR INDUSTRY THROUGH BEST PRACTICES THAT LEAD TO SUPERIOR PERFORMANCE

DESCRIPTION

This book was written on the premise that benchmarking is the key to becoming the best of the best. Readers will discover what benchmarking is, how benchmarking is performed, and what the results of successful applications are. Reference guides will help readers get started. Case histories provide examples of actual benchmarking investigations from beginning to end.

HOW DO I USE IT?

Benchmarking: The Search for Industry through Best Practices that Lead to Superior Performance contains the following sections: why to benchmark; what to benchmark; identifying competitive companies; data collection methods; determining the current competitive gap; projecting future performance levels; communicating benchmark findings; establishing functional goals; developing action plans; implementing specific actions; recalibrating; and beyond benchmarking.

COST

Available to ASQC members for $31.95 and to non-members for $34.95. Prices do not include shipping and handling.

STRENGTHS AND WEAKNESSES FOR USERS

The book is useful in that it provides the methodology of how to plan, implement, and measure a benchmarking project in all settings. The case histories allow the reader to better understand how benchmarking can successfully work in a variety of settings. The book is 299 pages long, so it should not be considered a "quick reference guide."

USER BASE

The book is available through the American Society for Quality Control (ASQC). With more than 130,000 individual members and 900 sustaining members, ASQC is one of the largest and most diverse professional organizations dedicated to quality.

USER SUPPORT

	N/A	Available	Comments
Consultants	x		
Documentation		x	
Training Classes		x	
Telephone Support	x		

VENDOR CONTACT

ASQC
P.O. Box 3005
Milwaukee, WI 53201-3005
VOICE   (800) 248-1946
URL   http://www.asqc.org

BUSINESS PARTNERING FOR CONTINUOUS IMPROVEMENT: HOW TO FORGE ENDURING ALLIANCES AMONG EMPLOYEES, SUPPLIERS AND CUSTOMERS

DESCRIPTION

Written by Charles C. Poirier and William F. Houser, *Business Partnering for Continuous Improvement: How to Forge Enduring Alliances Among Employees, Suppliers and Customers* shows how to make the drive for quality, productivity and profit improvement a permanent feature of any organization. The book draws on extensive studies of over 50 leading-edge companies to explain how business partnering works in practice with employees, suppliers and customers.

HOW DO I USE IT?

Business Partnering for Continuous Improvement: How to Forge Enduring Alliances Among Employees, Suppliers and Customers describes programs and results of such industry leaders as Toyota Motor Company, Amex Life, and Levi Strauss and Co. The book explains how to adapt these programs to small or large manufacturing or service companies.

COST

Available to CUED members for $29.95 and to non-members for $33.95.

STRENGTHS AND WEAKNESSES FOR USERS

The 256-page book offers the user a rich array of case studies to help form successful partnering relationships.

USER BASE

The book is available through the National Council for Urban Economic Development (CUED), a leading national organization serving economic development practitioners. CUED was founded in 1967 and currently has over 1,500 members.

USER SUPPORT

	N/A	Available	Comments
Consultants	x		
Documentation	x		
Training Classes	x		
Telephone Support	x		

VENDOR CONTACT

CUED
1730 K Street
Washington, DC 20006
VOICE   (202) 223-4735
FAX   (202) 223-4745

CYCLE TIME REDUCTION

DESCRIPTION

This tool is a self-audit checklist developed by consultant R. Michael Donovan to help companies reduce cycle time, inventories and costs. The assessment tool is designed to help companies identify and sidestep pitfalls and develop an action plan that will maximize results. The checklist focuses on the order-to-delivery cycle and covers management practices, customer focus, quality planning, employee involvement and teamwork, supplier relations and action planning.

HOW DO I USE IT?

The user makes copies of the checklist, distributes it to management personnel to fill out and assigns a coordinator to compile and summarize the responses. The management team meets to review the results and discuss how best to approach changes that will improve overall customer satisfaction and profit performance.

COST

The checklist is free.

STRENGTHS AND WEAKNESSES FOR USERS

The checklist is most useful as a tool to facilitate discussions among the management team and to develop consensus on management goals. It is 12 pages in length with mostly yes and no questions. Users may find it difficult to answer many of the questions with just a yes or no, but the purpose of the questions is to generate discussion on setting performance goals.

USER BASE

Users have included manufacturers of engineered machinery, mechanical equipment, metal products, and electronic equipment.

USER SUPPORT

	N/A	Available	Comments
Consultants		x	R. Michael Donovan, Inc. provides management consulting services for a fee.
Documentation		x	
Training Classes		x	
Telephone Support		x	

VENDOR CONTACT

R. Michael Donovan, Inc.
209 West Central Street
Natick, Massachusetts 01760-3716
VOICE   (508) 655-4100 or (800) 745-4101
FAX   (509) 655-3000

DIRECTORY OF ADVANCED MANUFACTURING CENTERS

DESCRIPTION

This directory is the first comprehensive listing of technical assistance centers for manufacturers. The centers provide a wide range of services to companies both large and small and to federal and state agencies. Fifteen hundred centers completed an 11-page survey that addresses services, budgets, client statistics, and manufacturing technologies.

HOW DO I USE IT?

The directory is produced in both hard copy and electronic forms. The electronic program consists of a menu that guides users through a selection process that produces manufacturing centers according to specific user needs. Individual center descriptions or entire center listings can be printed.

COST

NACFAM members: $120 for hardcopy, $140 for diskette.
Non-NACFAM members: $140 for hardcopy, $230 for diskette.

STRENGTHS AND WEAKNESSES FOR USERS

This is the most comprehensive listing of manufacturing centers available. Users can choose centers by desired capability, so it saves time. Each listing has a great deal of information about each center.

USER BASE

Not available.

USER SUPPORT

	N/A	Available	Comments
Consultants		x	
Documentation	x		
Training Classes		x	
Telephone Support	x		

VENDOR CONTACT

NACFAM
1331 Pennsylvania Ave., NW
Suite 1410-North
Washington, DC 20004-1703
VOICE   (202) 662-8960
FAX   (202) 662-8964

EMPLOYEE HANDBOOK OF NEW WORK HABITS FOR A RADICALLY CHANGING WORLD

DESCRIPTION

See listing in Human Resources section, page 24.

ENCOMPASS

DESCRIPTION

EnCompass, a product of EnCompass Technologies, Inc. (a Blue Marble Company), is a computer system for analyzing operations, processes, organizations, and communications and for synthesizing improvements and monitoring an organization's progress in these activities. *Encompass* captures detailed information from all important elements of the organization and integrates and displays the results in a visual and readily analyzed and communicated form. *Encompass* is the product of a collaborative effort of leading specialists in management systems and world-class expertise in visual data management and display.

How Do I Use It?

EnCompass can be hosted on 486 or Pentium personal computers or Power PCs operating under Windows, Windows 3.1, Windows 95, or OS/2. It can be configured as a client-server application compatible with standard SQL databases or as a stand-alone application. The methodology embodied in *EnCompass* has proven effective in addressing challenging problems in a broad spectrum of environments—industry, government, nonprofits and academia. The interactive nature of the system facilitates team processes, consensus building, and effective implementation of enduring solutions.

Cost

The price of the stand-alone configuration of *EnCompass* Version 2.0 is $30,000, which includes a report-writer and a day of application training. Leasing arrangements are also available. Discounted pricing for academic institutions for research and education applications.

Strengths and Weaknesses for Users

EnCompass makes effective use of familiar graphical user interfaces and the latest advances in visual information navigation and display to provide a user-friendly system with readily understood and communicated outputs. It provides well-thought-out default analyses to permit new and occasional users to effectively utilize the system quickly with a minimum of training, and it provides an extensive inventory of flexible and highly customizable analysis and synthesis tools to support the challenging requirements of the most sophisticated and experienced users. The effective use of *EnCompass* requires a willingness to openly and objectively assess business processes and a commitment to support the implementation of team-oriented, cross-functional concepts.

Lotus Development Corporation has recommended *EnCompass* to companies for developing templates for the installation of Lotus Notes systems. Ms. Judy Borck, CEO of Country Home, has used *EnCompass* to assist the management team in improving product development, manufacturing planning, and customer support. The Los Angeles Metropolitan Water District is using *EnCompass* to streamline critical parts of the agencies procurement system and to support internal TQM initiatives. It is being used by the Los Angeles County Sheriff's Department to redesign organizational structure and systems to improve resource utilization. National Semiconductor is using *EnCompass* to reengineer business systems and processes.

User Base

Since its introduction in the spring of this year, *EnCompass* has been adopted by a range of users including an international aerospace company, a national specialty food manufacturing and distribution company, an international freight forwarding company, and a major telecommunications company. In addition, it is being adopted by a number of progressive management and systems consulting firms to expand and enhance the services they provide to their clients.

USER SUPPORT

	N/A	Available	Comments
Consultants	x		
Documentation		x	
Training Classes		x	
Telephone Support	x		

VENDOR CONTACT

Dr. Michael Mann, CEO
EnCompass Technologies. Inc.
A Blue Marble Company
406 Amapola Avenue, Suite 200
Torrence, CA 90501
VOICE   (310) 328-3583
FAX   (310) 328-9057

FINANCIAL AND OPERATING RATIOS SURVEY

DESCRIPTION

See listing in Financing and Business Practices section, page 6.

INTERFIRM COMPARISONS

DESCRIPTION

InterFirm Comparisons (IFC) is a proven tool for benchmarking companies' competitive performance and recommending steps to improve their performance. It is both diagnostic and prescriptive. InterFirm comparative analysis identifies companies' competitive strengths and weaknesses in terms of a variety of performance measures which cover the full range of business performance including financial health, productivity, costs, profitability, quality, technology, management, sales and marketing. A business is viewed as an organism whose every part is related to every other.

HOW DO I USE IT?

A minimum of six comparable companies, all in the same segment of industry, must voluntarily elect to participate. Participating companies complete a set of standardized data collection forms directly from their records. The data are entered into a computer database. Some data are adjusted to ensure comparability of performance measures among the participants. Each participant supplying data receives comparative performance tables plus a customized report that interprets the results and makes recommendations for executives' actions.

COST

The cost can vary from $500 to $2,500 per company depending on two factors: 1) the number of participants (the more participants, the lower the cost); and 2) cost sharing between companies and any sponsors, such as industry trade associations, government agencies, and/or industry development organizations.

STRENGTHS AND WEAKNESSES FOR USERS

It is sometimes difficult to put together a set of comparable firms. The major weakness, however, becomes a strength through the *IFC* process—the fact that many companies do not have the data readily available to diagnose their performance. The *IFC* data collection format becomes the core of an improved management information system for monitoring company performance.

USER BASE

The users include electronics manufacturers, tool and die shops and other small-scale metalworking companies, precision metal stampers, and housewares producers and distributors.

USER SUPPORT

	N/A	Available	Comments
Consultants		x	Consultancy is included in the fixed price per company.
Documentation		x	Data collection forms, instructions and model reports included.
Training Classes	x		
Telephone Support		x	

VENDOR CONTACT

Development Strategies Corporation
47 Pleasant Street
Gloucester, MA 01930-5944
Attn: Peter Bearse, Ph.D., President or Chris Michaud, Office Manager
VOICE   (508) 281-6992
FAX   (508) 281-6588

ISO 9000 CHECKLIST

DESCRIPTION

ISO 9000 Checklist is a list of detailed questions based on the international quality management standard ISO 9001-1994. Companies and service providers can use this list to get an initial understanding of the systems a company already has in place, the systems that are in place but not documented, and the particular systems that need to be developed. The tool can help determine a firm's readiness for implementing an ISO 9000-compliant quality system.

How Do I Use It?

ISO 9000 Checklist is available in hard copy. A person familiar with ISO 9000 can complete it with assistance from company personnel knowledgeable about company systems (e.g., a quality manager, plant manager, or department heads). Time to complete is estimated at two hours, depending on the complexity of the company.

Cost

ISO 9000 Checklist costs $25 per copy. Quantity discounts are available.

Strengths and Weaknesses for Users

ISO 9000 Checklist gives a quick baseline for a company wondering what level of effort may be involved in becoming ISO 9000-compliant. It is based on ISO 9001 but can easily be adapted to 9002. Familiarity with ISO 9000 is not required but provides a better understanding of checklist results. Updates to the standard will necessitate updates to the checklist; the next update is scheduled for 1999.

User Base

Extension engineers and CISQ auditors in Georgia have been using this list as a tool to determine how to plan the path toward compliance with ISO 9000 standards.

User Support

	N/A	Available	Comments
Consultants	x		
Documentation	x		
Training Classes		x	Not required to use the checklist, but helpful for interpreting results. Call (800) 859-0968.
Telephone Support	x		

Vendor Contact

Donna Ennis, Marketing Manager
Center for International Standards & Quality (CISQ)
Georgia Tech Economic Development Institute
Atlanta, GA 30332-0640
VOICE   (800) 859-0968 or, in Atlanta area, (404) 853-0968
FAX   (404) 894-1192
E-MAIL   donna.ennis@edi.gatech.edu

ISO 9000 COURSE LICENSING PROGRAM

DESCRIPTION

The CISQ *ISO 9000 Course Licensing Program* is a cost-effective way to offer in-depth training to all members of a company's ISO 9000 implementation team, as well as an overview to all employees. Available CISQ courses cover three critical elements of ISO 9000 implementation:

- Basic knowledge of the ISO standards and the registration process;
- Internal quality auditing; and
- Documentation preparation.

Executive Introduction to ISO 9000 is a one-day seminar that is 65 percent lecture and 35 percent exercises. It is adaptable to various audiences, including senior and middle managers, supervisors, and operators. It gives a detailed overview of ISO 9000, examines the registration process, and offers an auditing exercise suitable for large or small groups.

ISO 9000 Internal Quality Auditing is a two-day workshop that is 40 percent lecture and 60 percent exercises. It presents auditing techniques, provides practical exercises based on actual firms' experiences, and prepares students to work effectively within a company audit program.

How to Prepare ISO 9000 Documentation is a two-day workshop that is 40 percent lecture and 60 percent exercises. It combines classroom exercises with unique teaching tools; presents and demonstrates documentation samples such as forms, checklists, flowcharts, and manuals based on real companies; and prepares students for the reality of documentation preparation.

Training of Trainers courses provide intensive instruction on how to conduct these CISQ courses. (See **ISO 9000 Training of Trainers** for more information.)

HOW DO I USE IT?

CISQ offers limited use of its high-quality training materials and innovative teaching tools. Each course comes with materials for instructors and students. Optional workshop materials are also available. A variety of choices gives the flexibility of creating a series of courses to fit a particular company's needs.

COST*

	Single-State	Multi-State
Executive Introduction to ISO 9000		
Basic Program	$3,750	$7,500
Discount Price**	$2,250	$4,500
ISO 9000 Internal Quality Auditing		
Basic Program	$7,500	$15,000
Discount Price**	$4,500	$9,000

How to Prepare ISO 9000 Documentation

Basic Program	$7,500	$15,000
Discount Price**	$4,500	$9,000

*   *Costs are current as of June 1995 and are subject to change.*

**   *Special 40 percent discount for nonprofit organizations and companies using the program for internal training only.*

STRENGTHS AND WEAKNESSES FOR USERS

Licensing of courses is a cost-effective way for companies with sizable internal training needs to train employees in the key areas of ISO 9000 while using minimal training dollars. The CISQ *ISO 9000 Course Licensing Program* is also a great income generator for businesses or organizations seeking to increase revenue. In addition to the presentation materials and student manuals, CISQ also provides an instructor's guide of essential points for each slide and other valuable information. Instructor training is also available for each course. Licensing of these courses would not be as valuable to small companies, for whom sending a small number of employees to open enrollment courses would be more cost-effective.

USER BASE

The Center for International Standards & Quality (CISQ) at Georgia Institute of Technology's Economic Development Institute has successfully tested these courses in Georgia and with U.S. industry. During the past year, CISQ has conducted these courses more than 60 times.

USER SUPPORT

	N/A	Available	Comments
Consultants	x		
Documentation		x	
Training Classes	x		Training of instructors available at additional cost.
Telephone Support	x		

VENDOR CONTACT

Donna Ennis, Marketing Manager
Center for International Standards & Quality (CISQ)
Georgia Tech Economic Development Institute
Atlanta, GA 30332-0640
VOICE   (800) 859-0968 or, in Atlanta area, (404) 853-0968
FAX   (404) 894-1192
E-MAIL   donna.ennis@edi.gatech.edu

ISO 9000 IMPLEMENTATION PROGRAM

DESCRIPTION

The CISQ *ISO 9000 Implementation Program* is a special outreach program designed to help small and medium-sized businesses develop and implement quality systems that conform to ISO 9000 standards. CISQ provides this program for license to service providers and large manufacturing firms desiring to conduct an *ISO 9000 Implementation Program* for companies in their region or for a group of suppliers to their firm. Under the licensing arrangement, CISQ provides training and materials, company assessment instruments, and training evaluation instruments. In the Program Management Training course, CISQ trains a company's service providers and supply liaison personnel to plan and conduct the implementation program, which is designed for 10 companies per group. Gap Analysis Training provides training and practice in the use of the detailed Gap Analysis Checklist used to determine a company's current documentation and information levels and to identify additional documentation and information needed to meet ISO 9000 requirements.

HOW DO I USE IT?

The CISQ *ISO 9000 Implementation Program* is designed to help groups of firms develop and implement a successful ISO 9000 registration strategy over a period of one year. It offers a variety of training and implementation assistance components including gap analysis, ISO 9000 in Detail, Train the Trainer, Internal Auditor training, Documentation workshops, and Pre-assessment Audits.

Program Management Training features a three-day course to train program managers and coaches in setting up and managing an Implementation Program, marketing the program, selecting participants, identifying resources, and solving problems.

Gap Analysis Training ensures that managers and coaches can effectively employ the detailed worksheet provided with the license for the Implementation Program. Proper use of this tool provides a rapid assessment of which ISO elements and sub-elements are already covered in available documentation and what remains to be written. It is a valuable tool for planning purposes.

COST*

License for the CISQ *ISO 9000 Implementation Program*, a series of training activities and active guidance for a selected group of companies over a period of 12 months.

Industry	$15,000
Nonprofit Organization	$8,500

Program Management Training for managers/coaches
(3-day course) $1,050 per person

Gap Analysis Training
Level 1 (2 days)	$700 per person
Level 2 (1 day)	$350 per person

* *Costs are current as of June 1995 and are subject to change.*

Strengths and Weaknesses for Users

Small companies seeking registration find it increasingly difficult to dedicate the time, personnel, and financial resources to the process required to achieve ISO 9000 compliance. The CISQ *ISO 9000 Implementation Program* provides a structured foundation with critically timed incentives to keep small companies moving forward. It is a strong revenue generator for organizations seeking to provide a *total* implementation assistance program to its customers. Service providers meet their assistance goals and large firms are able to bring a group of suppliers to maximum potential without major program development costs and without getting mired in potential pitfalls.

Success does hinge on instructors and coaching staff having strong knowledge of ISO 9000 and having adequate resources available to assist companies. Program Management Training provides the background, criteria, and approaches needed to quickly implement the *ISO 9000 Implementation Program*. Gap Analysis Training provides training in use of the detailed assessment tool included with the program.

User Base

The Center for International Standards & Quality (CISQ) at Georgia Institute of Technology's Economic Development Institute has successfully tested this program with 21 manufacturers in Georgia.

User Support

	N/A	Available	Comments
Consultants	x		
Documentation		x	
Training Classes		x	
Telephone Support		x	

Vendor Contact

Donna Ennis, Marketing Manager
Center for International Standards & Quality (CISQ)
Georgia Tech Economic Development Institute
Atlanta, GA 30332-0640
VOICE   (800) 859-0968 or, in Atlanta area, (404) 853-0968
FAX   (404) 894-1192
E-MAIL   donna.ennis@edi.gatech.edu

ISO 9000 Training of Trainers

Description

The CISQ *ISO 9000 Training of Trainers* provides intensive instruction on how to conduct the courses offered for licensing as *Executive Introduction to ISO 9000, ISO 9000 Internal Quality Auditing,* and *How to Prepare ISO 9000 Documentation.*

The program provides two levels of instructor training for organizations that license CISQ courses through the CISQ *ISO 9000 Course Licensing Program*. In an easy-to-understand format, Level 1 introduces participants to ISO 9000 and the non-lecture instructional techniques used in the training courses. It also offers an opportunity for participants to practice instructing the courses. Level 2 is for individuals who already have a high level of ISO 9000 knowledge, industry assistance experience, and non-lecture instructional techniques. It offers accelerated training modules that provide details on how the courses are designed and what questions commonly arise. Participants passing the written and practical exams for either level will receive Georgia Tech certification as an instructor.

How Do I Use It?

As soon as the licensing agreement is signed, a company's personnel are eligible to participate in the associated Training of Trainers course. Personnel selected to instruct a course should attend the appropriate Training of Trainers course prior to presenting the course. Classes are scheduled at least twice a year. Contact CISQ at (800) 859-0968 for the current schedule of classes.

Cost*

Executive Introduction to ISO 9000
    Level 1 (3 days) $1,050 per person
    Level 2 (1 day) $350 per person

ISO 9000 Internal Quality Auditing
    Level 1 (5 days) $1,750 per person
    Level 2 (2 days) $700 per person

How to Prepare ISO 9000 Documentation
    Level 1 (5 days) $1,750 per person
    Level 2 (2 days) $700 per person

* Costs are current as of June 1995 and are subject to change.

Strengths and Weaknesses for Users

Offering two levels of training directly meets the specific needs of potential course instructors, avoiding both insufficient and redundant information. While not essential to course presentation, the *ISO 9000 Training of Trainer Program* significantly accelerates instructor familiarization with each course. These courses are geared primarily to manufacturers but can be adapted to service or other industries.

User Base

The Center for International Standards & Quality (CISQ) at Georgia Institute of Technology's Economic Development Institute has successfully tested this program in Georgia.

USER SUPPORT

	N/A	Available	Comments
Consultants	x		
Documentation		x	
Training Classes		x	
Telephone Support		x	

VENDOR CONTACT

Donna Ennis, Marketing Manager
Center for International Standards & Quality (CISQ)
Georgia Tech Economic Development Institute
Atlanta, GA 30332-0640
VOICE   (800) 859-0968 or, in Atlanta area, (404) 853-0968
FAX   (404) 894-1192
E-MAIL   donna.ennis@edi.gatech.edu

LEAN MANUFACTURING—A SIMULATION

DESCRIPTION

Lean manufacturing is a manufacturing philosophy which, when implemented, shortens the time between customer order and factory shipment by eliminating waste. The University of Kentucky's Center for Robotics and Manufacturing Systems offers the *"Lean Manufacturing Simulation,"* in which participants work on a simulated factory floor and actually manufacture a product. This is a powerful hands-on approach designed to familiarize manufacturers with the concepts and benefits of this manufacturing method.

HOW DO I USE IT?

The simulation allows participants to develop a strategy for production improvement of a manufacturing operation using principles and practices based on: built-in quality, visual control, just-in-time, pull system, work leveling, continuous improvement and teamwork.

COST

The one day *"Lean Manufacturing Simulation"* is offered for $250 per participant—quantity discounts may apply. There is also a "Lean Manufacturing Executive Awareness Workshop for CEOs and Senior Managers," for which price quotes are available upon request.

STRENGTHS AND WEAKNESSES FOR USERS

The simulation offers users a reasonable-priced method to learn about lean manufacturing. Because the concepts under study involve a paradigm shift away from traditional manufacturing, some time and study will be required.

USER BASE

The University of Kentucky's Center for Robotics and Manufacturing Systems' lean manufacturing program has been developed with the cooperation of Toyota Motor Manufacturing U.S.A. CEOs, senior managers, operating managers, first level supervisors, technical support staff and production workers will find the simulation beneficial. The workshops are geared to the level needed for company executive, management, and support staff.

USER SUPPORT

	N/A	Available	Comments
Consultants	x		
Documentation		x	
Training Classes		x	Available at the University of Kentucky.
Telephone Support		x	

VENDOR CONTACT

Patricia G. Hammond
Engineering Professional Development
217 CRMS Building
University of Kentucky
Lexington, KY 40506-0108
VOICE   (606) 257-4295
FAX   (606) 323-1035

LEAN PRODUCTION USER GROUPS (LPUG)

DESCRIPTION

Lean Production User Groups (LPUG), a product of Rother & Company, is a system that brings together groups of manufacturers to impose a discipline of meeting regularly to analyze operations and develop ways to improve them. With the help of a facilitator, *LPUGs* focus on implementation of lean/synchronous manufacturing and associated management systems via a learn-by-doing approach. Both shopfloor and management employees are involved.

HOW DO I USE IT?

LPUGs are started through local manufacturers, associations, colleges and business-assistance groups. Interested companies or groups can contact Rother & Company; the company facilitates *LPUGs* and helps regional organizations develop their own *LPUG* programs.

A typical group is comprised of six companies that commit to one year of operation and pay a per-company membership fee. *LPUG* meetings are six weeks apart and occur at member plants. The host site rotates among members.

LPUG starts with a set of half-day executive meetings. Next, three to four employees from an area targeted for improvement at each member company attend a series of workshops. At each workshop, members critique one another's progress reports on the targeted projects, review a focus topic, and conduct an analysis on the host's shop floor. All *LPUG* meetings are conducted by a facilitator.

Cost

The cost to manufacturers for one year of *LPUG* membership ranges from $4,000 to $8,000 per member company depending on the scope of work and expenses involved. Rother & Company promotes transfer of the *LPUG* approach with temporary joint facilitation with interested organizations and has a fee structure for helping regional organizations build their own *LPUG* program.

Strengths and Weaknesses for Users

*LPUG*s offer a means to accelerate the adoption of lean production. The regular, facilitated meeting and reporting discipline promotes continued effort, and the group format provides experience-based suggestions and a real-world implementation orientation. *LPUG* members must commit to attending group meetings and to making application progress between meetings. *LPUG*s are not a seminar series to watch. Organizations wishing to start their own *LPUG* programs will need to provide a local contact person, who will be trained by Rother & Company.

User Base

Since 1990, approximately 18 *LPUG*s have been active in Illinois, Michigan, Minnesota, Mississippi, New Jersey, New York, and Ohio. More than 100 manufacturers have been involved. *LPUG*s are the subject of a recent *Wall Street Journal* article describing the approach and its impacts.

Organizations now using the *LPUG* approach include the New York City Industrial Technology Assistance Corporation, New Jersey Institute of Technology, the Applied Technology Center (Grand Rapids, MI), the Precision Metalforming Association, the Midwest Manufacturing Technology Center (Ann Arbor, MI), Delta Council (Stoneville, MS), and the Employer's Association (Sylvania, OH).

User Support

	N/A	Available	Comments
Consultants		x	
Documentation		x	
Training Classes		x	
Telephone Support		x	

Vendor Contact

Mr. Mike Rother
Rother & Company
429 Third Street
Ann Arbor, MI 48103
VOICE   (313) 665-5411

LEARNERFIRST: HOW TO IMPLEMENT ISO 9000

DESCRIPTION

This interactive software application helps a company understand and prepare for ISO 9000 registration. It personalizes the process by providing information one needs specifically for one's own organization. It breaks the complex registration process into simple, step-by-step activities. The new Q9000-1994 quality standards are integrated into this software program as a value-added reference tool.

The application will help one to select and implement an ISO standard, tailor the selected standard to the organization's needs, write a quality manual that will meet ISO standards, avoid the pitfalls of ISO registration, and meet the ISO 9000 requirements. *How to Implement ISO 9000* automatically enables one to successfully apply the standards to one's own company. One can also customize the standards, reducing the time spent on muddling through information.

HOW DO I USE IT?

The application helps one understand and prepare for ISO 9000 registration. It guides one to write a quality manual that will meet ISO standards, as well as help develop and implement an ISO 9000 plan. It follows an eight-step implementation process: 1) decide to proceed, 2) assess current position, 3) determine the shortfalls, 4) develop an implementation plan, 5) perform the documentation process, 6) manage transitional activities, 7) validate one's compliance to ISO, and 8) pass the registration audit. The application produces reports at the end of each activity. *LearnerFirst: How to Implement ISO 9000* can be used with an IBM personal computer or compatible with a 20 MHz 80386 or higher processor.

COST

This tool costs $695. Prices do not include shipping and processing.

STRENGTHS AND WEAKNESSES FOR USERS

The application provides an extensive database for collecting and maintaining document control and shortfall analysis. It provides everything one needs to know to prepare for the registration audit.

USER BASE

This tool can be used by companies preparing for ISO 9000 registration.

USER SUPPORT

	N/A	Available	Comments
Consultants	x		
Documentation		x	Comes with a 140-page user's guide.
Training Classes	x		
Telephone Support		x	LearnerFirst offers technical support by phone, fax, and e-mail.

VENDOR CONTACT

LearnerFirst, Inc.
1075 13th Street South
Birmingham, Alabama 35205
VOICE   (205) 934-9182
FAX   (205) 975-1037
E-MAIL   LearnFast@aol.com

LEARNERFIRST: PROCESS MANAGEMENT

DESCRIPTION

Every organization consists of hundreds of processes that either enhance or inhibit performance. This interactive, how-to software helps one to understand a particular organization's processes and then guides one in determining which processes to change and how to do it. It will help a company to increase process productivity to enhance profits and ensure higher levels of customer satisfaction. The experts at Tennessee Associates developed the four-stage process management methodology that leads a company through the entire improvement or re-engineering process. *LearnerFirst Process Management* software can be used for "clean sheet" process reengineering, high performance methodology, strategic planning and reporting, "questioning" methodology, process management training, team supplier-customer analysis, and ISO 9000 documentation.

HOW DO I USE IT?

Step-by-step tasks lead a company through the entire improvement process from beginning to end. The custom database organizes, saves, and analyzes organizational data, minimizing the work related to managing processes. Specific examples, dialogue questions, suggestions, guidelines and checklists are included to help one assess and improve the performance of the company's most critical processes.

COST

The cost is $445. Prices do not include shipping and processing.

STRENGTHS AND WEAKNESSES FOR USERS

Because learning is integrated with work, the user saves time by learning, doing, and documenting at the same time. The easy-to-use interface and dynamic illustrations make it easy to navigate through the application. Many useful reports are available.

USER BASE

Process Management is used by organizations, departments or teams to improve and perform better.

USER SUPPORT

	N/A	Available	Comments
Consultants	x		
Documentation	x		
Training Classes	x		
Telephone Support		x	LearnerFirst offers technical support by phone, fax, and e-mail.

VENDOR CONTACT

LearnerFirst, Inc.
1075 13th Street South
Birmingham, Alabama 35205
VOICE   (205) 934-9182
FAX   (205) 934-1037
E-MAIL   LearnFast@aol.com

MAPPING WORK PROCESSES

DESCRIPTION

This hands-on, step-by-step workbook outlines the creation of flowcharts. These flowcharts can help any work process. Detailed exercises teach anyone how to chart and document processes, understand them, and make improvements from them.

HOW DO I USE IT?

The 89-page workbook instructs the user in the creation of a flowchart through the following process: introduction to mapping; select the process; define the process; chart the primary process; chart the inspection points; develop inspection standards; draw arrows and lines; chart inputs and suppliers; chart subprocesses; and plan future activities. It is written in a straightforward manner and includes a summary of key points in each chapter.

COST

Mapping Work Processes is available for $13 to ASQC members and $15 to non-members. The price does not include shipping and handling.

STRENGTHS AND WEAKNESSES FOR USERS

The workbook is easy to follow. It tells how to create flow charts rather than why to create flow charts. It is simple and short but useful.

USER BASE

The book is available through the American Society for Quality Control (ASQC). With more than 130,000 individual members and over 900 sustaining members, ASQC is one of the largest and most diverse professional organizations dedicated to quality.

USER SUPPORT

	N/A	Available	Comments
Consultants	x		
Documentation		x	
Training Classes		x	
Telephone Support	x		

VENDOR CONTACT

ASQC
P.O. Box 3005
Milwaukee, WI 53201-3005
VOICE   (800) 248-1946
URL   http://www.asqc.org

OX-9000

DESCRIPTION

OX-9000 is a document management system specifically assembled to support ISO-9000 document management requirements. The *OX-9000* product includes software, a special hardware workstation, and specialized system integration.

HOW DO I USE IT?

OXKO delivers and installs the workstation on a client's local area network (LAN). OXKO trains a system administrator. The client then uses *OX-9000* to perform ISO-9000 documentation activities electronically.

COST

$50,000 per LAN, unlimited number of users, includes installation and training.

STRENGTHS AND WEAKNESSES FOR USERS

OX-9000 provides all ISO-9000 documentation management requirements. Users have commented that with some training and orientation, *OX-9000* greatly decreased the documentation activities required to obtain IS0-9000 certification.

USER BASE

There are three plants using *OX-9000* with over 1500 users cumulatively.

USER SUPPORT

	N/A	Available	Comments
Consultants		x	Some provided with purchase.
Documentation		x	Some provided with purchase.
Training Classes		x	Some provided with purchase.
Telephone Support		x	Some provided with purchase.

VENDOR CONTACT

Steven Oxman
OXKO Corporation
175 Admiral Cochrane Drive
Annapolis, MD 21401
VOICE   (410) 266-1671
FAX   (410) 266-6572

PUTTING TOTAL QUALITY MANAGEMENT TO WORK

DESCRIPTION

Putting Total Quality Management to Work: What TQM Means, How to Use It, and How to Sustain It Over the Long Run offers a compact resource to what total quality management means in practice. This 216-page guide outlines what organizations can and should do about TQM, identifying the keys to making it work on a long-term basis.

HOW DO I USE IT?

Putting Total Quality Management to Work details resources on major TQM tools, including control charts, flow charts and scatter diagrams. It also details criteria for the Baldrige National Quality Award and provides a list of key TQM information sources.

COST

Available to CUED members for $19.95 and to non-members for $23.95.

STRENGTHS AND WEAKNESSES FOR USERS

The guide provides practical guidance on how to use TQM tools and techniques, how the quality management process is rooted in the culture of the organization, and how leaders can build cultures that support and sustain TQM. At 216 pages, the publication is more than just a "quick guide."

USER BASE

The guide is available through the National Council for Urban Economic Development (CUED), a leading national organization serving economic development practitioners. CUED was founded in 1967 and currently has over 1,500 members.

User Support

	N/A	Available	Comments
Consultants	x		
Documentation	x		
Training Classes	x		
Telephone Support	x		

Vendor Contact

CUED
1730 K Street
Washington, DC 20006
VOICE   (202) 223-4735
FAX   (202) 223-4745

Quality Function Deployment: Linking a Company with Its Customers

Description

Quality Function Deployment: Linking a Company with Its Customers provides a step-by-step description of quality function deployment (QFD) and how QFD utilizes customer wants and needs to help product development. This book can be used to implement QFD as a means to increase an organization's competitiveness and develop a base of satisfied customers.

How Do I Use It?

The 245-page book contains the following sections: the QFD concept; overview of the QFD process; the voice of the customers; developing a QFD matrix; reviewing the matrix for priority items; deployment to subsequent levels—parts deployment; process deployment; manufacturing deployment; ancillary matrices with potential value; using the QFD concept in business planning; and organizing teams and planning QFD projects.

Cost

Available to ASQC members for $37 or $41 for non-members. Prices do not include shipping and handling.

Strengths and Weaknesses for Users

The book should be useful to organizations wishing to become more responsive to customer wants and needs. It shows how QFD applies to nonengineering settings.

User Base

The book is available through the American Society for Quality Control (ASQC). With more than 130,000 individual members and 900 sustaining members, ASQC is one of the largest and most diverse professional organizations dedicated to quality.

User Support

	N/A	Available	Comments
Consultants	x		
Documentation	x		
Training Classes	x		
Telephone Support	x		

Vendor Contact

ASQC
P.O. Box 3005
Milwaukee, WI 53201-3005
VOICE   (800) 248-1946
URL   http://www.asqc.org

Quick View

Description

Quick View is a business planning and assessment tool which provides the big picture of a manufacturer's operation's and competitive position. Originally intended to be a "self-help" tool, *Quick View* has filled a need for the growing number of extension programs nationally, looking for ways to accurately assess a manufacturers' needs and begin the improvement process. The major advantage of *Quick View* is that it focuses both the firm and the extension agent on the business areas that warrant further investigation to determine specific improvement projects. It is an excellent diagnostic tool for the firm that wishes to improve its competitive position but does not know where to start.

How Do I Use It?

The manufacturers fill out the questionnaire with assistance from the field staff or an MTC or other industrial assistance organization. Field staff generally introduce company personnel to the tool and help them interpret results.

Cost

Varies depending on the extension agency administering the questionnaire.

STRENGTHS AND WEAKNESSES FOR USERS

This tool is quick and easy to understand and takes about one hour to complete. The resulting output report compares the manufacturer against a database of similar firms that previously responded to the questionnaire.

A Company Profile report is generated that assesses 14 different areas of the manufacturer's operations: Management, Human Resources, Purchasing, Manufacturing Technology, Bidding, Documentation, Market Management, Quality, Engineering, Production Process, Communication, Information Systems, and Pollution Prevention and Waste Minimization.

The report uses an easy to read graphical format to represent the company's performance. In addition, the report indicates which response to which questions on the part of the firm led to low or high ratings. The report is not diagnostic but simply indicates the relative strengths and weaknesses of the firm in the 14 major business areas listed above. The report is designed to be presented to the firm by the local industrial extension agent who will then discuss the types of services that would be available to the firm through their agency. Turnaround time for processing is three to four days.

USER BASE

The tool can be used by any manufacturing firm with 50 to 500 employees. Over 1100 companies have participated to date. More than 30 MTCs use *Quick View*.

USER SUPPORT

	N/A	Available	Comments
Consultants	x		
Documentation		x	
Training Classes	x		
Telephone Support		x	

VENDOR CONTACT

New York Manufacturing Extension Partnership
385 Jordan Road
Troy, NY 12180-8347
Attn: Peter Petruccione
VOICE   (518) 283-1010
FAX   (518) 283-1112
E-MAIL   peter_petruccione@mailgate.nymep.nysstf.org

TBE—THE BENCHMARKING EXCHANGE

DESCRIPTION

The Benchmarking Exchange, or *TBE*, is a comprehensive and user-friendly electronic communication and information system designed specifically for use by individuals and organizations involved in benchmarking. *TBE* provides users with a comprehensive, centralized and specialized forum for all phases of benchmarking. *TBE* is for veteran practitioners as well as those who are just beginning to discover the world of benchmarking; it was designed by and for benchmarking practitioners. *TBE* features include:

- Best Practices Database;
- Posting Board communications center;
- Malcolm Baldrige National Quality Award library;
- benchmarking presentations and articles;
- upcoming events;
- member directory; and
- TBE e-mail.

HOW DO I USE IT?

To access *TBE*, one may use one's own communications software or let *TBE* provide free modem software for Windows, DOS, or Macintosh. One may access *TBE* via modem from 2,400-28,800 bps. On-line *TBE* service is available on the World Wide Web through the following URL: *http://www.benchnet.com*

COST

TBE is available for a flat rate of either $255 for three months, $495 for one year, or $745 for two years, with no initiation fees or additional costs.

STRENGTHS AND WEAKNESSES FOR USERS

TBE is designed with both the novice and expert in mind and is entirely menu-driven. Help functions are available throughout *TBE*, and the *TBE* help desk is staffed with professionals on weekdays.

USER BASE

TBE is the service of choice in both the private and public sectors. *TBE*'s members come from varying sizes of organizations and include:

- 47 percent of the Fortune 100 companies (latest 1995 ranking);
- 66 percent of the Malcolm Baldrige National Quality Award winners (latest 1995 award exam);
- 17 countries; and
- over 250 organizations.

USER SUPPORT

	N/A	Available	Comments
Consultants		x	
Documentation		x	
Training Classes	x		
Telephone Support		x	

VENDOR CONTACT

The Benchmarking Exchange, Inc.
7960-B Soquel Drive, Suite 356
Aptos, CA 95003
VOICE (408) 662-9800
FAX (408) 662-9801
E-MAIL admin@benchnet.com
URL http://www.benchnet.com

UNDERSTANDING QS-9000

DESCRIPTION

Understanding QS-9000 is a two-day introductory course to the new quality standard for the automotive industry. Quality System Requirements (QS-9000) is the result of the "best practice" selection of the supplier requirements from the Big Three automakers (Ford, Chrysler and General Motors). Its three sections include ISO 9000 requirements with annotations as required—requirements specific to the automotive sector and requirements specific to a particular customer. The course covers the first two sections in detail, as well as the registration process and system documentation. Hands-on practice is included throughout the course.

HOW DO I USE IT?

The course is presented on a regular basis in Atlanta by certified QS-9000 auditors from the Georgia Tech Center for International Standards and Quality (CISQ). The course can also be licensed for use.

COST

Cost of the two-day course is $695 per person. There is a $50 per person discount for multiple attendees. For on-site courses, travel expenses are additional.

STRENGTHS AND WEAKNESSES FOR USERS

Any current or future automotive supplier to Ford, Chrysler, or General Motors—or to any of their first-tier suppliers—will find this course valuable.

Compliance to QS-9000 is already required for all suppliers of production and service parts and materials to the Big Three automakers. Chrysler and General Motors will require registration to QS-9000 between 1996 and 1997. Ford has not yet set a deadline for registration.

CISQ has been presenting ISO 9000 courses since 1991 and has a history of providing quality training and technical assistance to industry. CISQ currently assists companies in gaining ISO 9000 registration and offers similar assistance to companies registering for QS-9000.

USER BASE

CISQ began presenting this course to automotive industry suppliers in October 1995. The course does not require knowledge of the ISO 9000 standard.

USER SUPPORT

	N/A	Available	Comments
Consultants		x	
Documentation		x	
Training Classes		x	
Telephone Support		x	

VENDOR CONTACT

Donna Ennis, Marketing Manager
Center for International Standards and Quality (CISQ)
Georgia Tech Economic Development Institute
Atlanta, GA 30332-0640
VOICE   (800) 859-0968 or, in Atlanta area, (404) 853-0968
FAX   (404) 894-1192
E-MAIL   donna.ennis@edi.gatech.edu

WORK PROFILING SYSTEM

DESCRIPTION

See listing in Human Resources section, page 57.

CHAPTER 5

REGULATORY

CLEAN PROCESS ADVISORY SYSTEM (CPAS™)

DESCRIPTION

CPAS™ is a collection of design software aimed at providing designers with the tools to include environmental considerations into product and process designs. Specific tools available in the 1996 release will provide information on available separation, pollution prevention, and treatment technologies with an emphasis on innovative technologies and case studies. Simulation software for the removal of organic contaminants from air and water by adsorption, and water by packed tower aeration, surface aeration, and diffuse bubble aeration is also included. Design ranking software will be included that can be used to incrementally evaluate process designs on an economic as well as environmental basis is included. Physical property database software is included for many solvents and other organic chemicals.

HOW DO I USE IT?

The software is designed for Microsoft® Windows™. Input requirements vary from one application to another but typically involve preliminary design specifications.

COST

Cost is dependent upon selection of tools purchased and level of involvement in tool development. Call (906) 487-3551 for current pricing information, or send e-mail to: cpas@mtu.edu

STRENGTHS AND WEAKNESSES FOR USERS

The software focuses on providing quick answers to design questions including an environmental consideration. This information will assist design engineers but is not intended to make design decisions.

CPAS™ is being developed as a collaborative project involving industrial and university consortia and federal agencies. Any interested parties are encouraged to become involved in the development of *CPAS™*.

USER BASE

The software is intended for use by anyone involved in the design process, including managers, design engineers, environmental specialists, and consultants.

USER SUPPORT

	N/A	Available	Comments
Consultants	x		
Documentation		x	
Training Classes	x		
Telephone Support		x	

VENDOR CONTACT

National Center for Clean Industrial and Treatment Technologies
Michigan Technological University
Houghton, MI 49931
VOICE   (906) 487-3143
FAX   (906) 487-3292

COMPLIANCE GUIDE FOR THE PROCESS SAFETY MANAGEMENT OF HIGHLY HAZARDOUS CHEMICALS IN THE PAINT INDUSTRY

DESCRIPTION

This manual, intended for paint and coatings manufacturers, describes developing a process safety management program. The program complies with Occupational Safety and Health Administration's (OSHA) final rule entitled the *Process Safety Management of Highly Hazardous Chemicals, Explosives and Blasting Agents*. The manual is produced by the National Paint and Coatings Association (NPCA).

HOW DO I USE IT?

The information contained in the manual has been developed from interpretations provided by OSHA. Contents include an introduction to the process safety management standard, employee participation, process safety information, process hazard analysis, operating procedures, incident investigation, emergency planning and response, and compliance audits.

COST

Members of NPCA, $55. Non-members, $480.

STRENGTHS AND WEAKNESSES FOR USERS

In April of 1995, the NPCA's Safety and Loss Prevention Subcommittee published a supplement to the guide. This supplement expands determination and evaluation of hazard analysis methods, and adds a new program guidance section and OSHA contact information.

USER BASE

NPCA is a voluntary, nonprofit trade association representing some 500 paint and coatings manufacturers, raw materials suppliers, and distributors. Collectively, NPCA's membership produces approximately 75 percent of the total dollar-volume of paints and industrial coatings sold in the United States.

USER SUPPORT

	N/A	Available	Comments
Consultants	x		
Documentation	x		
Training Classes	x		
Telephone Support	x		

VENDOR CONTACT

National Paint and Coatings Association
1500 Rhode Island Avenue, NW
Washington, DC 20005
VOICE   (202) 462-6272
FAX   (202) 462-8549

DEALING WITH PROPOSITION 65— COMPLIANCE AND ENFORCEMENT ISSUES

DESCRIPTION

This issue analysis booklet covers background and compliance information concerning Proposition 65, also known as the Safe Drinking Water and Toxic Enforcement Act of 1986. The booklet gives an overview of Proposition 65's principal objectives, chemical review processes, warning requirements, chemical discharge prohibitions, enforcement practices, and other key attributes and requirements. The majority of the booklet outlines necessary company considerations regarding clear and reasonable warning requirements that are associated with consumer product, occupational, and environmental exposures.

HOW DO I USE IT?

The booklet is designed to help companies develop a Proposition 65 compliance program.

COST

Free.

STRENGTHS AND WEAKNESSES FOR USERS

In addition to this issue analysis booklet, other National Paint and Coatings Association (NPCA) resources featuring information on California's Proposition 65 are also available.

USER BASE

NPCA is a voluntary, nonprofit trade association representing some 500 paint and coatings manufacturers, raw materials suppliers, and distributors. Collectively, NPCA's membership produces approximately 75 percent of the total dollar-volume of paints and industrial coatings sold in the United States.

USER SUPPORT

	N/A	Available	Comments
Consultants	x		
Documentation	x		
Training Classes	x		
Telephone Support	x		

VENDOR CONTACT

National Paint and Coatings Association
1500 Rhode Island Avenue, NW
Washington, DC 20005
VOICE   (202) 462-6272
FAX   (202) 462-8549

DON'T BE ALARMED...BE AWARE!

DESCRIPTION

This video program has been specifically prepared for tooling and machining job shops in order to address compliance with hazard communication training regulations. Included with the video is a detailed leader's guide and a set of employee workbooks. These written materials, in combination with the videotape, provide an easy, systematic way of meeting Occupational Safety and Health Administration's (OSHA) requirements and protecting employees from chemical hazards. The program can be used with groups of employees or for individual training. It comes with 25 workbooks and a supply of employee quizzes and documentation forms. Extra materials are available. Reference materials are also included in the package, including a list of OSHA offices.

HOW DO I USE IT?

The training program comes with a leader handbook. The training program itself consists of videotape instruction, workbooks, and exercises.

COST

The program costs $89.95 for National Tooling and Machining Association (NTMA) members, and $179.95 for the general public.

Strengths and Weaknesses for Users

The combination of videotape and written exercises make an effective learning format. Tips and suggestions for the program leader help ensure proper management of the training. The cost for such a comprehensive program is reasonable.

User Base

NTMA consists of more than 3,000 tooling and machining companies in 56 chapters throughout the U.S. Sixty-five percent of the members have 20 employees or less.

User Support

	N/A	Available	Comments
Consultants	x		
Documentation		x	
Training Classes		x	
Telephone Support	x		

Vendor Contact

The National Tooling & Machining Association
9300 Livingston Road
Ft. Washington, MD 20744
VOICE   (301) 248-6200
FAX   (301) 248-7104

FESA Library CD-ROM Regulatory Database

Description

The *Federal Environmental and Safety Authority (FESA) Library CD-ROM Regulatory Database* integrates all current Federal Register information with multiple CFR titles 10, 21, 29, 30, 33, 40, and 49—all on one CD-ROM. The database also contains multiple state coverages, and over 40 regulatory compliance manuals and guidance materials from the Occupational Safety and Health Administration (OSHA) and the Environmental Protection Agency (EPA). Users can import database text and tables into any word processor with few reformatting changes. Flexible subscription options are available.

How Do I Use It?

The database runs on 386 or 486 microcomputers with VGA monitors and CD-ROM players. DOS or Windows versions are available.

Cost

$495 to $2,500 annually, depending on subscription frequency.

STRENGTHS AND WEAKNESSES FOR USERS

With this database, users can find regulatory compliance regulations with a push of a few keys instead of looking through volumes of paper.

USER BASE

Users of the database include over 500 small-to-large firms such as Monsanto, Motorola, Quaker Oats, and General Electric.

USER SUPPORT

	N/A	Available	Comments
Consultants	x		
Documentation		x	
Training Classes		x	
Telephone Support	x		

VENDOR CONTACT

Attn: Paul Thormodsgard
Citation Publishing, Inc. (CPI)
1435 N. Hayden Road
Scottsdale, AZ 85257
VOICE (602) 994-4560
FAX (800) 808-3372

THE HAZARDOUS MATERIALS IDENTIFICATION SYSTEM (HMIS®)

DESCRIPTION

The Hazardous Materials Identification System (HMIS®) is a compliance aid aimed at employers who need a simple, comprehensive way to communicate chemical hazards to employees.

HOW DO I USE IT?

Text for the system includes: 1) a plain-language introduction to chemical hazard communication; 2) extensive information on understanding and evaluating compliance with Occupational Safety and Health Administration's (OSHA) 1994 revised Hazard Communication Final Rule; 3) procedures and guidelines for producing *HMIS®* ratings materials; 4) information on producing Material Safety Data Sheets, including information on the optional American National Standards Institute Z400.1 format; 5) a side-by-side comparison of *HMIS®* and NFPA® labeling systems; 6) a question and answer appendix to frequently asked *HMIS®* questions; and 7) an expanded glossary including common acronyms, MSDS terminology, health hazard definitions, and conversion factors. The publication is sponsored by the National Painting and Coating Association (NPCA).

COST
Contact vendor.

STRENGTHS AND WEAKNESSES FOR USERS
Enhancements to this revised edition include: 1) modified health rating criteria that improves the recognition of chronic hazards and reinforces the usage of asterisks as a way of identifying all chemicals clearly associated with chronic health effects to employees; 2) updated flammability and reactivity rating criteria contained in the latest edition of the National Fire Protection Association (NFPA)® 704 *Recommended System for the Identification of the Fire Hazards of Materials*; and 3) more flexible PPE options, allowing employers to create their own PPE combinations.

USER BASE
NPCA is a voluntary, nonprofit trade association representing approximately 500 paint and coatings manufacturers, raw materials suppliers, and distributors. Collectively, NPCA's membership produces approximately 75 percent of the total dollar-volume of paints and industrial coatings sold in the United States.

USER SUPPORT

	N/A	Available	Comments
Consultants	x		
Documentation	x		
Training Classes	x		
Telephone Support		x	

VENDOR CONTACT
Labelmaster
5724 N. Pulaski Road
Chicago, IL 60646
VOICE   (800) 621-5808

INDUSTRIAL SOLID WASTE WORKBOOK

DESCRIPTION
This in-depth workbook helps local government and industry reduce the amount of solid waste going into landfills. Based on the concept of focus groups, the workbook provides worksheets and data sheets as a self-assessment tool. The worksheets determine the quantity and true cost, including conversion factors, of all types of solid waste. It lists common alternatives to disposal for major solid waste types.

HOW DO I USE IT?

The book leads users through a Solid Waste Reduction Assessment. By referring to tables and filling out worksheets, the user develops a description of solid waste streams at a facility, quantities generated and cost estimates, the operations or processes that generate these wastes, a list of specific and general suggestions for waste reduction, sources for additional technical information, and information needed to develop and implement a continuing waste reduction program. Users may need training and support, but the workbook can stand alone as an assessment tool. The appendices contain lists of Tennessee recycling resources.

COST

This tool is free.

STRENGTHS AND WEAKNESSES FOR USERS

Not everything contained in the workbook will apply to all users. Revisions of the workbook are planned, and the workbook will be updated periodically. It does not rank or develop costs of alternatives. Although the workbook is based on Tennessee law, it is useful in meeting federal guidelines as well. The elements of a written facility plan are based on the Environmental Protection Agency's voluntary "program in place."

USER BASE

The workbook was developed for the more than 6,500 Tennessee manufacturing firms.

USER SUPPORT

	N/A	Available	Comments
Consultants		x	To Tennessee companies only.
Documentation		x	
Training Classes		x	To Tennessee companies only.
Telephone Support		x	

VENDOR CONTACT

University of Tennessee
Center for Industry Studies
226 Capitol Boulevard, Suite 606
Nashville, TN 37219
Attn: Keith Ridley
VOICE   (615) 532-4928
FAX   (615) 532-4937

Lockout for Safety, Lockout for You!

Description

Managers develop an Occupational Safety and Health Administration-mandated lockout program and train employees in lockout procedures with this easy-to-use training program. Topics covered include: introduction to lockout, basic lockout rules, lockout requirements, when lockout is not needed, hazardous information energy found in a typical metalforming company, seven steps for lockout, removing lockout, transferring lockout responsibilities, and outside contractors. The complete training system includes easy-to-follow instructions, a two-part VHS videotape, a manager's guide (with sample written lockout program), performance tests, lockout decals, lockout posters, and completion certificates.

How Do I Use It?

Training is easy with the Precision Metalforming Association's (PMA) unique VIEW/ReVIEW Training Systems. The systems are unique self-paced learning programs that place the responsibility for learning on the individual employee and minimize interruptions. With PMA video training systems, employees learn what they need to know to be safer and more productive. "Refresher courses" and new employee training are hassle-free because the program stays on-site.

Cost

The first set of the system costs $295 for PMA members, with additional sets costing $150. The first set of the system costs $595 for the general public, with additional sets costing $450.

Strengths and Weaknesses for Users

Users move at their own pace through the training materials. The system uses several media—VHS videotapes, written exercises, and text—to teach the course. Several materials specific to the lockout subject are included in the package including decals, posters, and completion certificates. Materials are focused on the metalforming industry.

User Base

The Precision Metalforming Association represents the $31 billion metalforming industry of North America—the industry that gives utility to sheet metal by shaping it using tooling machines. The membership consists of more than 1,200 companies including metal stampers, fabricators, spinners, and roll formers, as well as suppliers of equipment, materials, and services to the industry.

User Support

	N/A	Available	Comments
Consultants	x		
Documentation		x	
Training Classes	x		
Telephone Support	x		

VENDOR CONTACT

The Precision Metalforming Association
27027 Chardon Road
Richmond Heights, OH 44143
VOICE   (216) 585-8800
FAX   (216) 585-3126

MANAGING CHEMICAL HAZARDS

DESCRIPTION

This videotape addresses compliance with environmental regulations affecting tooling and machining job shops. The goal is to make companies in this industry aware of environmental legislation that has been passed at the federal, state, and local levels. The tape, targeted at company owners and managers, presents an overview of the various environmental regulations of Environmental Protection Agency (EPA) and Occupational Safety and Health Administration (OSHA), as well as strategies that ensure compliance.

The tape reviews the six primary federal environmental laws that affect tooling and machining companies:

1) The Emergency Planning and Community Right-To-Know Act, also known as SARA Title III;
2) The Hazard Communication Standard, more commonly known as the Right-To-Know Law;
3) The Clean Water Act which regulated the wastewater discharge to the nation's water resources and, in some cases, municipal sewer systems;
4) OSHA's In-Plan Air Quality Regulations;
5) The EPA's Underground Storage Tank Program; and
6) The Resource Conservation and Recovery Act.

HOW DO I USE IT?

The information is delivered by VHS videotape. The tape lasts approximately 20 minutes.

COST

The videotape costs $29.95 and is only available to National Tooling and Machining Association members.

STRENGTHS AND WEAKNESSES FOR USERS

The product offers a good overview of industry-specific regulations for tool and die shops. By its very nature, it is not a detailed how-to program for the industry.

User Base

NTMA consists of more than 3,000 tooling and machining companies in 56 chapters throughout the U.S. Sixty-five percent of the members have 20 employees or less.

User Support

	N/A	Available	Comments
Consultants	x		
Documentation	x		
Training Classes		x	
Telephone Support	x		

Vendor Contact

The National Tooling & Machining Association
9300 Livingston Road
Ft. Washington, MD 20744
VOICE   (301) 248-6200
FAX   (301) 248-7104

Paint Industry Labeling Guide—Fourth Edition

Description

This National Paint and Coatings Association (NPCA) manual focuses on paint and coatings industry labeling regulations and guidance. The manual provides recommendations for creating a label suitable for both retail and industrial markets.

How Do I Use It?

This guide recommends labeling practices while conveying an understanding of the appropriate principles of label creation. Chapters include a step-by-step approach to the principles of labeling systems, illustrations of precautionary statements, sample labels, label statements for conforming to industry practices and federal, state, and local laws, information on the U.S. Environmental Protection Agency's requirements for registering pesticides, and a glossary of labeling terms.

Cost

NPCA members, $100. Non-members, $900.

Strengths and Weaknesses for Users

A new guide supplement is scheduled for publication and includes updated health and safety information, and current revisions to federal and state laws and regulations.

USER BASE

NPCA is a voluntary, nonprofit trade association that represents approximately 500 paint and coatings manufacturers, raw materials suppliers, and distributors. Collectively, NPCA's membership produces approximately 75 percent of the total dollar-volume of paints and industrial coatings sold in the United States.

USER SUPPORT

	N/A	Available	Comments
Consultants	x		
Documentation	x		
Training Classes	x		
Telephone Support		x	

VENDOR CONTACT

National Paint and Coatings Association
1500 Rhode Island Avenue, NW
Washington, DC 20005
VOICE   (202) 462-6272
FAX   (202) 462-8549

POLLUTION PREVENTION TRAINING REPORT AND MODEL CURRICULUM

DESCRIPTION

This report provides users with information on how to establish a facility pollution prevention training program. It was developed by the Connecticut Technical Assistance Program (ConnTAP). ConnTAP is part of the Connecticut Hazardous Waste Management Service, a nonregulatory, quasi-public organization with statutory responsibility to promote multi-media pollution prevention in Connecticut. The report is intended to assist companies in the state with training workers on the importance of pollution prevention, from both environmental and economic standpoints. ConnTAP also makes the report available to companies outside the state.

HOW DO I USE IT?

The report is organized into two parts. The first part presents a case study demonstrating how a company developed and implemented pollution prevention training at its facility. The second part outlines a model pollution prevention training curriculum. The model curriculum was developed on lessons in the case study. The program can be adapted by the user to meet the needs of many types of companies. The model curriculum contains four training sessions, ranging from defining "pollution prevention" to developing a company pollution prevention plan. Within each session, a goal is established and then activities are presented to reach the goal. A bibliography containing resources for additional information is also included.

COST
The tool is free from ConnTAP.

STRENGTHS AND WEAKNESSES FOR USERS
This report provides an overview of pollution prevention training curriculum. Through a bibliography of additional resources and the presentation materials, employees can develop an effective curriculum that is targeted specifically to their needs. A major step for businesses wanting to reduce generation of pollution is to educate workers about the benefits of pollution prevention. An effective pollution prevention training program can achieve this important objective.

USER BASE
Not available.

USER SUPPORT

	N/A	Available	Comments
Consultants	x		ConnTAP provides technical assistance to companies in Connecticut. ConnTAP is also available to answer questions about the manual.
Documentation		x	
Training Classes	x		
Telephone Support		x	

VENDOR CONTACT
ConnTAP
50 Columbus Boulevard, 4th Floor
Hartford, CT 06106
Attn: Robert Brown, Technical Specialist
VOICE   (203) 241-0777
FAX   (203) 244-2017
E-MAIL   p2eline@aol.com

SAGE

DESCRIPTION
SAGE (Solvent Alternatives Guide), developed by Research Triangle Institute in cooperation with the Air and Energy Research Engineering Lab of the Environmental Protection Agency, assists

employees faced with selecting alternatives to existing solvent-based cleaning processes. *SAGE* asks the user a series of questions. The user selects one or more answers from a given menu. After the users answer the questions, *SAGE* provides a list of recommended alternatives. The information provided with each alternative includes general information about the specific chemistry or process, an environmental/safety section, a case study/economics section, and a section that lists contacts and references.

How Do I Use It?

SAGE is designed to operate on a 286 or higher IBM or compatible personal computer. The program is currently not available in an Apple Macintosh version. After the program is downloaded, on-line instructions prompt the user. The user does not need to be familiar with database search and retrieval techniques.

Cost

SAGE is available free-of-charge from the Control Technologies Center of the U.S. Environmental Protection Agency. It can be downloaded to a personal computer by calling (919) 541-5742 (9600-N-8-1).

Strengths and Weaknesses for Users

The greatest strength of *SAGE* is that it provides unbiased information on the various alternatives. *SAGE* will not recommend specific products or equipment; ultimately, users must determine the selection of a given alternative for a specific cleaning application.

User Base

The system is designed to be used by shop owners, state technical assistance offices, and anyone with questions about solvent substitution for metal degreasing and cleaning. More than 1000 copies have been downloaded since *SAGE* first became available in February 1993.

User Support

	N/A	Available	Comments
Consultants	x		
Documentation		x	Program is downloaded with "Readme.txt" in file. Help and step-by-step instructions are included on-line in the program.
Training Classes	x		
Telephone Support		x	A hotline operator can be reached at (919) 541-0800. Vendors may also be contacted for questions and user comments.

Vendor Contact

Mr. Chuck Darvin, AEERL
U.S. EPA

Research Triangle Park, NC 27709
VOICE   (919) 541-7633

Mr. Ken Monroe
Center for Environmental Technology
Research Triangle Institute
Research Triangle Park, NC 27709
VOICE   (919) 541-6916

SELF-AUDIT MANUAL FOR METAL FINISHERS

DESCRIPTION

This manual provides companies with a starting point for examining their facilities and minimizing hazardous waste. It was developed by the Connecticut Technical Assistance Program (ConnTAP), a program of the Connecticut Hazardous Waste Management Service. ConnTAP is intended to help Connecticut companies prevent pollution, save money by reducing treatment and disposal costs, and help limit liability by minimizing hazardous waste generation. ConnTAP makes the manual available to companies outside the state.

HOW DO I USE IT?

The manual is organized into three sections. The first section is a guidance document on establishing a waste minimization program, good operating practices in electroplating, and waste minimizing techniques. The information and data collection part of the document organizes the tasks of defining baseline conditions in facilities. The first section also includes a general facility questionnaire on recent compliance history and financial information necessary to calculate the current costs of waste management.

The second section consists of a Process Line Overview which should be completed for all facility process lines. The third section consists of Process Information sheets for all facility processes. These sheets can be grouped with their respective process line overview sheets. This section also consists of sheets for evaluating current and future waste minimization and recovery practices. The appendix provides conversion charts, information on a simplified process flow and material balance, and other assessment criteria.

COST

The tool is free from ConnTAP.

STRENGTHS AND WEAKNESSES FOR USERS

This manual provides a very detailed self-assessment. The worksheets organize cost and process information. The tables provide useful information to calculate material balance. Metal finishers should benefit from the manual even if they do not have the expertise to proceed beyond the data collection phase of an audit. The cost of hiring an outside consultant for such an audit can be greatly reduced if the metal finisher can provide well-organized baseline data.

USER BASE

Not available.

USER SUPPORT

	N/A	Available	Comments
Consultants		x	ConnTAP provides technical assistance to companies in Connecticut. They are available to answer questions about the manual.
Documentation		x	
Training Classes	x		
Telephone Support		x	

VENDOR CONTACT

ConnTAP
50 Columbus Boulevard, 4th Floor
Hartford, CT 06106
Attn: Robert Brown, Technical Specialist
VOICE   (203) 241-0777
FAX   (203) 244-2017
E-MAIL   p2eline@aol.com

SPILL & RELEASE ADVISOR

DESCRIPTION

Spill & Release Advisor is a microcomputer expert system that assists employees in determining if a chemical spill or release needs reporting to government agencies like the National Response Center. The *Advisor* covers regulations associated with CERCLA, SARA, UST, RCRA, and others.

HOW DO I USE IT?

The *Advisor* is loaded onto a microcomputer. When a need for assistance occurs, a user starts the program. The *Advisor* asks questions and the user provides answers about the chemical incident. When the *Advisor* has enough information, it provides recommendations.

COST

General public, $12,000. National Tooling and Machining Association members, $10,000.

STRENGTHS AND WEAKNESSES FOR USERS

The Advisor quickly provides regulatory information relevant to incident reporting requirements. Users have stated that the *Advisor* has made the incident reporting regulations easier to manage.

USER BASE

Approximately 200 copies of *Spill and Release Advisor* are in use.

USER SUPPORT

	N/A	Available	Comments
Consultants		x	Needed only if customization is required.
Documentation		x	Not usually necessary.
Training Classes		x	Not usually necessary.
Telephone Support		x	Not really necessary.

VENDOR CONTACT

Steven Oxman
OXKO Corporation
175 Admiral Cochrane Drive
Annapolis, MD 21401
VOICE   (410) 266-1671
FAX   (410) 266-6572

WASTE REDUCTION ASSESSMENT FOR THE FABRICATED METAL PRODUCTS INDUSTRIES

DESCRIPTION

This manual gives an overview of waste reduction for the fabricated metal products industry. It focuses on identifying solvent wastes, paint-related wastes, spent solvents, used oils, metal-working fluids, wastewaters, sludges, corrosive wastes, packaging wastes, metal wastes, and coolants. The manual also provides a guide to writing a waste reduction plan.

HOW DO I USE IT?

This manual provides information needed to conduct a self-assessment. To accomplish waste reduction, users first identify and characterize the waste stream. The first section describes the most common waste streams found in metal fabricating operations, along with regulatory requirements and other issues. The next section focuses on waste reduction options for individual waste streams including source reduction, disposal, and recycling. It offers suggestions to reduce waste through better operating practices and process modifications. Substitute cleaning agents and solvents are suggested. An appendix lists selected vendors for solvent recovery, parts cleaners, as well as recyclers and recovery facilities. A guide to writing a waste reduction plan helps meet the requirements of the Tennessee Hazardous Waste Reduction Act of 1990, but the guide is useful to all companies who can realize improvements in productivity, quality, and safety by reducing hazardous waste. The guide includes a waste reduction assessment checklist, a suggested outline, and general suggestions on writing the plan. A sample of a mock company's waste reduction plan is included.

COST
This tool is free.

STRENGTHS AND WEAKNESSES FOR USERS
The manual is a useful source of information on waste reduction for metalworking companies. It identifies waste streams produced by metalworking companies against which companies can identify their own waste streams. Some of the information on regulations is useful only to Tennessee companies, but the overall information is useful to any company needing to perform a waste reduction assessment.

USER BASE
Not available.

USER SUPPORT

	N/A	Available	Comments
Consultants		x	To TN companies only.
Documentation		x	
Training Classes		x	To TN companies only.
Telephone Support		x	

VENDOR CONTACT
University of Tennessee
Center for Industry Studies
226 Capitol Boulevard, Suite 606
Nashville, TN 37219
Attn: Keith Ridley
VOICE   (615) 532-4928
FAX   (615) 532-4937

WRITING A WASTE REDUCTION PLAN

DESCRIPTION
This handbook is a reference tool that shows how to review waste operations, identify and assess reduction options, and implement and measure progress. Providing businesses with practical infor-

mation on how to approach, plan, and implement a hazardous waste reduction program, the handbook motivates industry for administrative, material, or technological changes that result in less waste. The handbook gives an overview of the waste reduction process, as well as steps for self-assessment. It focuses on developing waste reduction policies, goal statements, and ways to establish performance goals, and it helps establish ways to monitor year-to-year waste reduction. The handbook gives an overview of Tennessee law, but the information is generic and applies to all waste reduction plans.

How Do I Use It?

Users create a plan to reduce waste at a facility. Managers perform the assessment by using a team approach. The guide is organized around nine elements of a successful program: 1) obtaining management commitment; 2) defining scopes, objectives, and goals; 3) conducting a waste assessment; 4) tracking the wastestreams; 5) evaluating waste reduction options for technical and economic feasibility; 6) implementation; 7) measuring results; 8) using a team approach; and 9) long-term commitment. Some training and support may be needed, but the manual can stand alone as an assessment tool by following the nine steps.

Cost

This tool is free.

Strengths and Weaknesses for Users

Because the needs of individual industries vary widely, companies may need to modify procedures discussed in the manual to meet their unique requirements. The book serves as a point of reference, not a set of rigid requirements. Although the handbook is based on Tennessee law, it is useful in meeting federal guidelines as well. The elements of a written facility plan required by Tennessee law are based on the EPA's voluntary "program in place."

User Base

Not available.

User Support

	N/A	Available	Comments
Consultants		x	To Tennessee companies only.
Documentation		x	
Training Classes		x	To Tennessee companies only.
Telephone Support		x	

Vendor Contact

University of Tennessee
Center for Industry Studies
226 Capitol Boulevard, Suite 606
Nashville, TN 37219
Attn: Keith Ridley
VOICE   (615) 532-4928
FAX   (615) 532-4937

CHAPTER 6

TECHNOLOGY

BEST MANUFACTURING PRACTICES (VOLUME 3)

DESCRIPTION

Best Manufacturing Practices is made up of the complete proceedings from the Precision Metalforming Association's 1993 Technical Symposium. Leading metalforming experts offer practical solutions to some of the toughest problems in more than 600 pages of ideas and information steeped in metalforming knowledge.

HOW DO I USE IT?

The text includes key facts, figures, and illustrations covering creative tooling, process improvements, management issues, and material and equipment subjects.

COST

Best Manufacturing Practices is available at a special price of $30 plus $5 shipping and handling per copy while supplies last.

STRENGTHS AND WEAKNESSES FOR USERS

The text offers a detailed look at metalforming issues and best practices from PMA's Technical Symposium at METALFORM '93. The text particularly focuses on process improvement.

USER BASE

The Precision Metalforming Association (PMA) represents the $31 billion metalforming industry of North America. Its more than 1,300 member companies include metal stampers, fabricators, spinners, and roll formers, as well as suppliers of equipment, materials, and services to the industry.

USER SUPPORT

	N/A	Available	Comments
Consultants	x		
Documentation	x		
Training Classes	x		
Telephone Support	x		

VENDOR CONTACT

PMA
27027 Chardon Road
Richmond Heights, Ohio 44143
VOICE   (216) 585-8800
FAX   (216) 585-3126

Best Manufacturing Practices Program: Sharing Best Practices Between Government, Industry, and Academia

Description

The *Best Manufacturing Practices Program* (BMP) is a sharing program that makes certified Best Manufacturing Practices available to the general public via print, Internet, diskette, CD-ROM, or BMPnet (their own network). These practices are the result of more than 80 on-site plant visits to gather and review manufacturing information. The objective of these plant surveys is to identify the best practices being used in the areas of design, testing, production, facilities, logistics, and management.

In addition, BMP has developed many useful software tools based on these best practices. These tools can be used to minimize risk during the product development process and provide critical information to aid in solving manufacturing problems. These software tools are: *SpecRite*, a performance specification development tool; *KnowHow*, an electronic library of expert systems on systems engineering; the ever-growing database of best practices; and *TRIMS*, a risk mitigation system. Taken together, this family of expert systems is commonly referred to as the *Program Manager's Workstation* (*PMWS*). The *PMWS*, the bulletin board for Special Interest Groups (SIG) in manufacturing, and many other network services are available free-of-charge on the BMP Network.

How Do I Use It?

You can ask for and receive survey reports from specific surveys or you can browse the network using the free software or via the program's home page on the World Wide Web. Also, the entire system is available on a CD-ROM that includes the on-line network database plus many expert systems tools developed in the program.

Cost

The CD-ROM costs $40, and the remaining services are free to the user.

Strengths and Weaknesses for Users

You must have access to either an IBM-compatible or Macintosh computer to make full use of the information and tools that BMP offers to its users.

User Base

The BMPnet is accessed more than 70,000 times per year.

User Support

	N/A	Available	Comments
Consultants		x	
Documentation		x	

	N/A	Available	Comments
Training Classes		x	
Telephone Support		x	

VENDOR CONTACT

The Best Manufacturing Practices Center of Excellence
4321 Hartwick Road, Suite 308
College Park, MD 20740
VOICE   (301) 403-8100
FAX   (301) 403-8180
BMPnet   (703) 538-7697
BMP Help Desk (703) 538-7253
E-MAIL   bmpinfo@bmpcoe.org
URL   http://www.bmpcoe.org

BMPNET

DESCRIPTION

BMPnet is a DOS-based dial-up network for the engineering and manufacturing communities. It contains the Program Manager's Workstation (PMWS), a suite of tools designed to help a program manager guide a development program through the complicated systems engineering process of design, development, and production. The workstation currently consists of four tools which are described in detail in this catalog individually: *SpecRite*, *KnowHow*, *TRIMS*, and the *BMP Database*. In addition, *BMPnet* provides for communication via e-mail, chat, and a SIG bulletin board, as well as information on the BMP Program.

HOW DO I USE IT?

Users can access *BMPnet* by using the communication program ONLAN, on an DOS-based personal computer with a modem.

COST

Free to industry and government personnel (Continental U.S. only).

STRENGTHS AND WEAKNESSES FOR USERS

PMWS is based on the Critical Path Templates, which provides a comprehensive framework for systems engineering, and current best practices from industry that have been collected and qualified by the BMP Program within the Navy.

USER BASE

Current user base is represented by the annual call volume on BMPnet, recently over 70,000 calls per year.

USER SUPPORT

	N/A	Available	Comments
Consultants		x	
Documentation		x	
Training Classes		x	
Telephone Support		x	

VENDOR CONTACT

BMP COE
4321 Hartwick Road, Suite 308
College Park, MD 20740
VOICE   (301) 403-8100
FAX   (301) 403-8180
BMPnet   (703) 538-7697   BMP Help Desk   (703) 538-7253
E-MAIL   bmpinfo@bmpcoe.org   URL   http://www.bmpcoe.org

BOILER EFFICIENCY PROGRAM

DESCRIPTION

The *Boiler Efficiency Program* is a stand-alone, DOS-based program using BAIER software. The program can be used to evaluate boiler combustion efficiency, water treatment effectiveness, blowdown operation, stack economizers, and blowdown heat recovery. Inputs of stack oxygen and temperature from a combustion test and selected water tests are required to run the program.

HOW DO I USE IT?

The *Boiler Efficiency Program* can be used on IBM or compatible computers (286 or higher). The program is menu-driven. After loading, the user selects the INPUT option and enters combustion and water quality data. The boiler combustion efficiency and conservation opportunity data calculated is then displayed and can be printed.

COST

The *Boiler Efficiency Program* is available for $450 and includes the software disk and a two-hour training session.

STRENGTHS AND WEAKNESSES FOR USERS

This program is quite useful for a specialized niche of users.

USER BASE

The *Boiler Efficiency Program* has been used primarily by Georgia Tech personnel to produce approximately 90 boiler survey audits. The software has been distributed to more than 30 industry users outside the Institute.

USER SUPPORT

	N/A	Available	Comments
Consultants	x		
Documentation		x	Software documentation is provided with software.
Training Classes		x	A two hour training session is included in the price.
Telephone Support	x		

VENDOR CONTACT

Michael Brown
Georgia Tech Economic Development Institute
O'Keefe Bldg., Rm. 209
Atlanta, GA 30332
VOICE   (404) 874-6107
FAX   (404) 853-9172
E-MAIL   mike.brown@edi.gatech.edu

BUSINESS GOLD BULLETIN BOARD

DESCRIPTION

The National Technology Transfer Center offers an electronic bulletin board that is accessed either directly through modem or via the Internet. It provides on-line information on federal technology available for licensing, a portion of federal databases, The Directory of Federal Laboratories, and Small Business Innovation Research program solicitations.

HOW DO I USE IT?

Business Gold may be accessed by modem by dialing (304) 243-2561 for 300-2400 baud or (304) 243-2560 for 9600 baud modems or higher. On the Internet, Telnet to the following: iron.nttc.edu. First time sign-ons should login as "guest." For help, call (304) 243-2551. NTTC also offers a World Wide Web site at: *http://www.nttc.edu.*

COST

The service is free. Users pay only for telephone tolls.

STRENGTHS AND WEAKNESSES FOR USERS

This service allows a one-stop, comprehensive source of federal technology information that is of interest to business. Because the information is public, no charges other than phone services are involved. As with most large databases, the size of *Business Gold* means that user difficulty increases.

USER BASE

Users of *Business Gold* include manufacturers and high tech companies, Small Business Development Centers (SBDCs), Technical Assistance Programs (TAPs), and research and development firms.

USER SUPPORT

	N/A	Available	Comments
Consultants	x		
Documentation		x	
Training Classes	x		
Telephone Support		x	

VENDOR CONTACT

Chuck Monfradi
National Technology Transfer Center
316 Washington Avenue
Wheeling, WV 26003
VOICE   (304) 243-2551
FAX   (304) 243-2539
E-MAIL   webmaster@nttc.edu

CADD SKILL STANDARDS DOCUMENT

See listing in Human Resources section, page 17.

CLEAN PROCESS ADVISORY SYSTEM (CPAS ™)

See listing in Regulatory section, page 124.

COALITION FOR INTELLIGENT MANUFACTURING SYSTEMS (CIMS)

DESCRIPTION

Monthly *CIMS* newsletters and reports include timely information on the 10-year global Intelligent Manufacturing Systems (IMS) Partnership, an international effort in the pursuit of manufacturing excellence. The reports include information on the progress of research projects underway; opportunities to join emerging projects; expressions of interest from U.S. and international organizations together with a full description of their capabilities and interests; and benchmarking studies and other related topics.

HOW DO I USE IT?

The newsletter is approximately 12 pages in length and is mailed monthly. An index and description of all other IMS reports is available through the *CIMS* office. Potential users can order from the index those reports which are of interest.

COST

Newsletters and reports are free to *CIMS* members. Newsletters are only available to *CIMS* members. Selected reports are available to non-members at costs ranging from $5-$100.

STRENGTHS AND WEAKNESSES FOR USERS

The newsletters and reports offer a comprehensive source of information on the IMS Partnership and the technologies emerging from ongoing IMS projects. They link users directly to the IMS community network by providing contact information and descriptions of capabilities and interests.

USER BASE

CIMS consists of over 40 member companies, trade associations, and research consortia who share an interest in intelligent manufacturing systems. The global IMS community network consists of hundreds of similar organizations from Australia, Canada, the European Union, Japan, and the United States.

USER SUPPORT

	N/A	Available	Comments
Consultants	x		
Documentation		x	
Training Classes	x		
Telephone Support		x	

VENDOR CONTACT

The Coalition for Intelligent Manufacturing Systems
1400 Eye Street N.W., Suite 540

Washington, DC 20005
VOICE   (202) 638-4434
FAX   (202) 296-1074
E-MAIL   rwsa@access.digex.net

Coil Fed Press Operator and Die Setter Training

Description

This video tool is a training system produced by the Precision Metalforming Association (PMA). It teaches coil fed press operators and die setters how to operate and set up coil fed presses in an easy-to-learn format. Topics include: component identification; proper dress and operator control of the press; operator controls of uncoilers, straighteners, and feeds; coil handling procedures; operating existing setups and adverse coil/material conditions; loading coils into existing setups; indicators of incorrect operation; measuring and gauging piece parts; changing progressive and blanking dies; uncoiling and straightening procedures; air operator and grip feeds; mechanical roll feeds; and producing the first part.

How Do I Use It?

The system includes easy-to-follow instructions, 12 VHS videotapes, an operator manual, a manager manual, a supervisor manual, a grader manual, written job aides to provide additional information and supporting materials too complex for the videotapes, and completion certificates.

Cost

The cost is $3,600 for PMA members for the first set and $600 for each additional set. The cost to non-members is $7,200 for each set. Shipping and handling is $15 per set.

Strengths and Weaknesses for Users

This tool provides needed training for new employees and refresher courses for others. It requires full management backing and participation.

User Base

The Precision Metalforming Association (PMA) represents the $31 billion metalforming industry of North America. Its more than 1,300 member companies include metal stampers, fabricators, spinners, and roll formers, as well as suppliers of equipment, materials, and services to the industry.

User Support

	N/A	Available	Comments
Consultants	x		
Documentation	x		
Training Classes	x		
Telephone Support	x		

VENDOR CONTACT
PMA
27027 Chardon Road
Richmond Heights, Ohio 44143
VOICE   (216) 585-8800
FAX   (216) 585-3126

COMMUNITY OF SCIENCE

DESCRIPTION

The *Community of Science* produces, maintains, and distributes a database of the same name, which is a comprehensive directory of research expertise, inventions, and facilities at leading U.S. and Canadian research universities, laboratories, and research and development organizations.

In addition, the *Community of Science* publishes "Federally-Funded Research in the U.S.," which consists of the entire grants databases of the National Institutes of Health (NIH), National Science Foundation (NSF), United States Department of Agriculture (USDA), and Small Business Innovation Research (SBIR). The company also publishes World Wide Web versions of the *Commerce Business Daily* (CBD) and *Federal Register*.

HOW DO I USE IT?

The *Community of Science* databases are fully-searchable on the World Wide Web (WWW) at *http://cos.gdb.org*. In addition, the company publishes a CD-ROM every quarter and also makes its databases available via modem with a telnet search interface.

COST

The company charges a flat annual fee to universities and other research institutions which supply data to the database. Corporate subscriptions are available for an annual fee for unlimited access. For companies with annual revenues under $25 million, the charge is $1,500 per year.

STRENGTHS AND WEAKNESSES FOR USERS

The *Community of Science* offers access to individual researchers performing advanced research in a number of scientific disciplines. This information is most appropriate for research universities and companies which are involved in leading-edge R&D and product development.

USER BASE

The *Community of Science* offers distributed access to researchers at dozens of major R&D companies and numerous research universities and nonprofit R&D organizations. More than 25,000 information transactions are processed each day on the WWW server alone.

USER SUPPORT

	N/A	Available	Comments
Consultants		x	
Documentation		x	Documentation is available for all three user interfaces.
Training Classes		x	The Community of Science frequently visits clients and prospective clients on-site, and also hosts an Annual Workshop for institutional liaisons.
Telephone Support		x	The Community of Science has an 800-number Helpline.

VENDOR CONTACT

Community of Science, Inc.
1615 Thames Street, Suite 104
Baltimore, MD 21231
Attn: Edwin Van Dusen
Vice President, Marketing and Operations
VOICE   (410) 563-5382
FAX   (410) 563-5389
E-MAIL   evd@bestpl.hcf.jhu.edu

COMPETITIVE TECHNOLOGY ASSESSMENT

DESCRIPTION

The *Competitive Technology Assessment (CTA)* report, produced by Mogee Research & Analysis Associates, assesses a firm's worldwide standing in a technology. The assessment is based on patenting data, including international patent families and patent citations. Active companies are ranked on level of activity in the technology, significance of their technological work, and how broadly they patent their inventions around the world. Changes in leadership over time are also traced. Companies are classified according to the length of their involvement in the technology. Major companies active in the technology are identified, and the client company's position is compared to that of the major competitors. This includes an analysis of the technology strategies being pursued by the client and major competitors. All of this is placed in the context of global trends and life-cycle stage of the technology.

HOW DO I USE IT?

The *Competitive Technology Assessment* is offered as a consulting service. To have a *CTA* done, contact the company. It will work with the customer to define the technology and determine the analysis and deliverable that will meet his or her needs.

COST

Costs range from $2800 for a single component of the *Competitive Technology Assessment* without a written report to $11,650 for the full assessment with written report and follow-up briefing. Data costs are charged separately and may range from $200 to $5,000, depending on the size of the technology.

STRENGTHS AND WEAKNESSES FOR USERS

The *CTA* is international in coverage (it covers the U.S. and approximately 30 other major industrialized countries). It identifies all companies that patent in a technology and characterizes their technological activity, and it integrates a broad range of statistics and analysis into a framework that allows a firm to see where it stands with respect to competitors and other companies active in a technology. It can be useful for technologies in which a company is active and those in which it is considering investing. The *CTA* may be especially appropriate for industrial or trade associations, extension services, and other organizations that serve small companies. It is not an effective tool for nonpatented technologies—e.g., software.

USER BASE

Not available.

USER SUPPORT

	N/A	Available	Comments
Consultants		x	The CTA is offered as a consulting service.
Documentation	x		
Training Classes		x	Classes on Patent Analysis can be arranged.
Telephone Support	x		

VENDOR CONTACT

Mary Ellen Mogee, Ph.D.
President
Mogee Research & Analysis Assoc.
11701 Bowman Green Drive
Reston, VA 22090
VOICE   (703) 478-2827
FAX   (703) 478-2827
E-MAIL   mogee@gwuvm.gwu.edu

CRITICAL TECHNOLOGY/INDUSTRIAL BASE ASSESSMENTS

DESCRIPTION

Critical Technology/Industrial Base Assessments are a series of in-depth reports designed to assess the health and competitiveness of sectors and technologies deemed vital to U.S. economic and national security. Initiated by the Department of Commerce's Bureau of Export Administration in its Strategic Analysis Division, each assessment was conducted using a mandatory industry survey, thereby offering industry information not otherwise available.

HOW DO I USE IT?

Designed for industry executives and government policymakers, each assessment provides comprehensive information and analysis on the production and technology status, economic performance and international competitiveness of private sector firms. While the Department of Defense has deemed the technologies and sectors studied essential to the development of the next generation of weapon systems, they are also crucial to the nation's ability to compete in the global economy.

COST

The assessments are available for sale through the National Technical Information Service and range in price from $55-$95 per report. The assessments range from 50-150 pages in length. Twenty-three assessments are publicly available (see master list) and three are underway—semiconductor materials infrastructure, small explosives, and software industries.

STRENGTHS AND WEAKNESSES FOR USERS

The assessments provide the reader with information regarding: Product Coverage and Applications, Financial Performance, Employment Trends, Shipments, Research and Development, Investment, Operations, Competitiveness, and more.

USER BASE

The Bureau of Export Administration's Strategic Analysis Division is the focal point within the Department of Commerce for developing, promoting, and implementing policies that ensure a strong, technologically superior defense industrial base.

USER SUPPORT

	N/A	Available	Comments
Consultants	x		
Documentation		x	
Training Classes	x		
Telephone Support		x	

VENDOR CONTACT

U.S. Department of Commerce
Bureau of Export Administration
SAD Room 3878

To order Assessments:
National Technical Information Service (NTIS)
Sales Desk (703) 487-4650

Washington, DC 20230
VOICE   (202) 482-4060
FAX   (202) 482-5650
E-MAIL   bbotwin@doc.gov

NTIS Rush Order Desk (800) 553-NTIS

CRYSTAL BALL

DESCRIPTION

Crystal Ball is a user-friendly, graphically oriented Monte Carlo simulation tool for risk analysis and forecasting. It operates on spreadsheet models and allows the user to specify any of 16 different input distribution types. It supports host spreadsheet functions, and optionally provides Latin Hypercube sampling. Results may be displayed as either line, area, or column histograms that show the likelihood of any given result. Version 3.0 includes a sensitivity chart for depicting relative importance between input distributions. *Crystal Ball* is a seamless add-in for Excel Versions 4.0 & 5.0, and Lotus 1-2-3, versions 4.0 & 5.0. It operates under Windows on the DOS-based personal computer, while the Macintosh product is for Excel only. Available since 1988, *Crystal Ball* has become one of the leading add-in products for Microsoft Excel.

HOW DO I USE IT?

Crystal Ball is to be used as an add-in to the spreadsheet programs Excel and Lotus 1-2-3. *Crystal Ball* is designed to perform risk analysis and forecasting based on a company's spreadsheet models.

COST

The product cost is $295

STRENGTHS AND WEAKNESSES FOR USERS

The product is very easy to use and user-friendly. It does not require statistical background. The user can generate impressive reports that will back sound, decision-making processes.

USER BASE

Not available.

USER SUPPORT

	N/A	Available	Comments
Consultants		x	
Documentation		x	
Training Classes		x	
Telephone Support		x	

VENDOR CONTACT

Decisioneering, Inc.
2530 S. Parker Road, Suite 220

Aurora, CO 80014
Attn: Saeed Hamid
VOICE   (303) 337-3531 or
            (800) 289-2550
FAX   (303) 337-3560

(DEPARTMENT OF ENERGY) DOE TECHNOLOGY INFORMATION NETWORK (DTIN)

DESCRIPTION

The *DOE Technology Information Network (DTIN)* is a searchable technology database on the WWW/Internet designed to help users from the technical business community find potential partners at DOE Laboratories and facilities for technology development. *DTIN* contains information on scientific and technical capabilities, research areas of individual staff members and technical groups, equipment and facilities available for external use, technologies available for licensing and commercial development, mechanisms for laboratory-industry partnerships, and federal funding opportunities.

HOW DO I USE IT?

To access *DTIN*, a user requires a personal computer with an Internet link and a World Wide Web browser such as Netscape™, Mosaic™, or a commercial provider connection such as CompuServe or America OnLine. The Internet URL address is: *http://www.dtin.doe.gov.*

Users can easily search *DTIN* by entering their request in free text or using a Boolean format. There is "Help" section for first-time users.

COST

There is no cost to use and search *DTIN*. All information is free to the public.

STRENGTHS AND WEAKNESSES FOR USERS

DTIN's strength is in the enabling information it contains and its search mechanism. Information contained in the *DTIN* system is continuously being updated and non-relevant information removed. As information considered important to users is identified, this information is being added daily.

DTIN's weakness is that not all DOE facilities are on-line. As each facility develops its unique capabilities information, it is being added to *DTIN*. The goal is to have the majority of labs and facilities on-line by the end of 1996. Users can fill out an on-line request for technical assistance or make other types of requests through the network. A comments e-mail form is also available on *DTIN*.

USER BASE
DTIN currently contain capabilities information from seven of 30 labs and facilities. All labs and facilities will be available in the future.

USER SUPPORT

	N/A	Available	Comments
Consultants		x	
Documentation		x	
Training Classes	x		
Telephone Support		x	

VENDOR CONTACT
Linda L. Rowton
Industrial Partnership Office
Los Alamos National Laboratory
P.O. Box 1663
Los Alamos, New Mexico 87545
VOICE   (505) 665-3322
FAX   (505) 667-0603
E-MAIL   lrowton@lanl.gov

DIMENSIONAL VARIATIONS IN FLAT ROLLED METALS

DESCRIPTION
This training series from the Precision Metalforming Association (PMA) covers key aspects of diagnosing problems with flat rolled material, as well as identifying causes and possible corrective actions. It includes information on thickness variations, coil set, cross bow, buckles, edge wage, twist, camber, surface defects, and proper material receiving and handling. Lesson #7 on Material Handling is available separately.

HOW DO I USE IT?
The system includes seven videotaped lessons ranging from 15 to 25 minutes in length. It also includes VIEW/ReVIEW trainee worksheets and performance checks.

COST
Shape Up!—Flat Rolled Metals and *Dimensional Variations—Causes and Corrections* are available to PMA members at $895 for the first set and $295 for additional sets. For non-members, each set is $1,790. Lesson #7 costs $145 for the first tape, $45 for additional tapes. Shipping is $15 per set.

STRENGTHS AND WEAKNESSES FOR USERS

The training series will likely not be of interest for the entire metalworking industry. It may prove valuable though to those working with flat rolled metals. The combination of videotapes, checklists, and worksheets should make for effective use in training. Cost may be high for small companies that are not PMA members.

USER BASE

PMA represents the $31 billion metalforming industry of North America. Its more than 1,300 member companies include metal stampers, fabricators, spinners, and roll formers, as well as suppliers of equipment, materials, and services to the industry.

USER SUPPORT

	N/A	Available	Comments
Consultants	x		
Documentation	x		
Training Classes	x		
Telephone Support	x		

VENDOR CONTACT

PMA
27027 Chardon Road
Richmond Heights, Ohio 44143
VOICE (216) 585-8800
FAX (216) 585-3126

ENERGY CONSERVATION TECHNICAL BRIEFS

DESCRIPTION

Energy Conservation Technical Briefs (Tech Briefs) are four-page flyers describing various contemporary energy-efficient technologies. Each Tech Brief contains a brief introduction to the technology, a detailed description of variations, applications, savings, a vendor list, and a glossary of terms. The following *Tech Briefs* are available:

1. Industrial Lighting
2. Solid State Motor Controls
3. Computer-Based Energy Management
4. Coal Technologies for Georgia Industry
5. High Pressure Nozzles
6. Direct Digital Control
7. Process Uses for Fluidized Beds
8. Cogeneration: A Georgia Option?

9. Fuel Cell Power Plants
10. Microwave Heating and Drying?
11. Automatic Boiler Blowdown
12. Industrial Ultrafiltration
13. Reducing Fluorescent Lighting Costs
14. Refrigerant Subcooling
15. Desiccant Air-Conditioning
16. Power Factor Correction Saves Energy

How Do I Use It?

Each *Tech Brief* contains sufficient detail to present a conservation technology and educate the reader in its application. Based on its contents, a reader will be able to determine if an advanced technology can be utilized in their facility.

Cost

A full set of 16 Tech Briefs costs $80.

Strengths and Weaknesses for Users

Tech Brief reports are sufficiently detailed to present the advantages, disadvantages, and potential applications for the subject technologies. Users must be familiar with a *Tech Brief* subject to be able to select a technology that could apply to their situation.

User Base

Tech Briefs have been supplied to state industries on an as-needed basis.

User Support

	N/A	Available	Comments
Consultants	x		
Documentation	x		
Training Classes	x		
Telephone Support	x		

Vendor Contact

Michael Brown
Georgia Tech Economic Development Institute
O'Keefe Bldg., Rm 209
Atlanta, GA 30332
VOICE   (404) 874-6107
FAX   (404) 853-9172
E-MAIL   mike.brown@edi.gatech.edu

ENERGY TIPS

DESCRIPTION

Energy Tips are one-page descriptions of low-cost/no-cost ways to save energy in industrial plants. Each tip has a graph, chart, or sample calculation to help determine potential energy savings. A total of 40 tips are available. Tips address the broad areas of lighting, boilers, compressed air, motors, and general process recommendations. The following IEES *Energy Tips* are available:

1. Steam Cost Chart
2. Eliminate Steam Leaks
3. Inspect and Repair Steam Traps
4. Insulate Bare Steam Lines
5. Boiler Tune-Up
6. Install Traffic Doors on Frequently Used Openings
7. Night Setback of Space Temperature
8. Keep Boiler Tubers Clean (Water Side)
9. Cover Heated Open Vessels
10. Return Steam Condensate to Boiler
11. Minimize Operating Pressure of Compressed Air Systems
12. Install Compressor Air Intakes in the Coolest Locations
13. Eliminate Leaks in Compressed Air Lines
14. Reuse Hot Wash Water
15. Recover Heat from Textile Dryer Exhaust Systems
16. Additional Effects Reduce Evaporator Steam Cost
17. Use Refuse as Fuel
18. Convert to More Efficient Light Source
19. Convert to Energy Efficient Fluorescent Lamps
20. Flashing High Pressure Condensate to Regenerate Low Pressure Steam
21. Minimize Boiler Blowdown
22. Reduce Reflux Ratios in Distillation Columns
23. Heat Recovery from Boiler Blowdown
24. Use Liquified Gases as Refrigerant
25. Reduce Energy Losses Across Control Valves
26. Skylights Provide Free Illumination
27. Vapor Recompression Can Reduce Steam Costs
28. Heat Recovery from Boiler Flue Gases
29. Use Low Grade Waste Heat to Power Absorption Refrigeration Units
30. Move Electric Motors from Air Conditioned Spaces
31. Air Curtains Restrict Conditioned Air Loss
32. Install Dock Seals to Reduce Heating Expenses
33. Reduce Airflow by Controlling Fan Speed
34. Install Reflectors in Fluorescent Light Fixtures
35. Install Electronic Ballasts in Fluorescent Light Fixtures

36. Use Vent Condenser to Capture Flash Steam Energy
37. Use Lowest Cost Fuels in Combustion Equipment
38. Use High Efficiency Motors
39. Improve Energy Efficiency of Exit Signs
40. Control Lighting with Occupancy Sensors

How Do I Use It?

Select an *Energy Tip* related to one's particular area of concern. The tip describes the energy loss problem and presents a solution. By referring to a related graph, chart, or sample calculation, the projected energy savings can be determined. The tips are self-explanatory, and no training is necessary.

Cost

A set of 40 *Energy Tips* costs $40.

Strengths and Weaknesses for Users

The *Energy Tips* clearly present numerous feasible conservation opportunities. The users must have significant understanding of their operation in order to effectively analyze the tip for their plant. The tips do not contain very detailed information on implementation costs.

User Base

Energy Tips are used by Georgia Tech engineers to aid in the preparation of energy audits, and they are distributed to plant personnel with questions about tip-related technology.

User Support

	N/A	Available	Comments
Consultants	x		
Documentation	x		
Training Classes	x		
Telephone Support	x		

Vendor Contact

Michael Brown
Georgia Tech Economic Development Institute
O'Keefe Bldg., Rm 209
Atlanta, GA 30332
VOICE (404) 874-6107
FAX (404) 853-9172
E-MAIL mike.brown@edi.gatech.edu

EXPERT CHOICE

DESCRIPTION

Expert Choice is a decision-support software tool based on methodology known as the Analytic Hierarchy Process (AHP). Ken Kleinberg, research director of The Gartner Group, has commented, "(It) relies on the user's ability to organize their problems in a hierarchy of goals and decision factors, and to judge the relative importance and effect of these factors in relation to each other. The method is particularly effective when the decision involves multiple, conflicting criteria and many possible courses of action. By requiring users to structure their problems in a hierarchy and make pairwise comparisons between factors (deriving rations), the AHP is able to draw out the often subjective nature of decision-making in a form that can be evaluated, modified, and documented. *Expert Choice* is able to combine judgments between factors into a unified whole, and thus is able to present users with ranked alternatives that represent a more formalized representation of both their intuitive and quantified decision-making."

HOW DO I USE IT?

AHP is the subject of numerous books, more than a thousand academic research papers, and many conferences and training programs. Typical applications of AHP involve evaluating options, ranking and selecting alternatives, allocating resources, and determining the likelihood of predictions. AHP can be used to improve group decision-making, to improve consistency of judgments, and to assist users in determining the sensitivity of decision factors.

COST

Expert Choice for Windows is available in many different versions: Trial ($20), Student (from $70), Educational ($416.50), Professional ($595), Network ($1995), and Runtime ($1995). Each product is supported by free technical support and a 30-day, money-back guarantee.

STRENGTHS AND WEAKNESSES FOR USERS

Expert Choice, Inc. has been the market leader in AHP-based software since 1983. It offers consulting and facilitation services, AHP software seminars, international symposiums, newsletters, and a CompuServe forum. While *Expert Choice* software is easy-to-use and straight forward, the concepts of AHP in building hierarchical decision models is an art that requires practice. However, the rewards of accurate and reliable decisions far outweigh the time invested in understanding some basic AHP concepts.

For example, IBM used Expert Choice on its Application System/400 (AS/400) Project to help win the Malcolm Baldridge Quality Award. As documented in the book *The Silverlake Project*, IBM needed a process to use for benchmarking, and they found Expert Choice to be the perfect tool: "(The AHP) enabled us to deal with our situation in all its complexity. Automated in the form of a relatively inexpensive software program called *Expert Choice*, AHP is an extraordinarily powerful decision-making tool."

USER BASE

Expert Choice has 15,000 installations to date and is used in more than 15 countries worldwide.

USER SUPPORT

	N/A	Available	Comments
Consultants		x	Wide range of custom and configured consulting packages.
Documentation		x	Full manual provided with software purchase, plus many books on AHP for sale.
Training Classes		x	Seminars are held two to three times a year with additional classes given on a consulting basis.
Telephone Support		x	Expert Choice has free technical support and a CompuServe forum.

VENDOR CONTACT

Expert Choice, Inc.
5001 Baum Blvd.
Suite 650
Pittsburgh, PA 15213
VOICE   (412) 682-3844
FAX   (412) 682-7008
E-MAIL   sales@ahp.net
URL   http://ahp.net/www/ahp/
CompuServe ECISUPPORT

GATEWAY

DESCRIPTION

Gateway is a free service for business and industry callers to access technology, research-in-progress, expertise, and unique facilities at more than 700 federal laboratories as well as federally funded research conducted at universities.

HOW DO I USE IT?

Gateway is easily accessible by calling (800) 678-6882. Customer service representatives will take incoming requests which will then be assigned to technology access agents. This (800) line is available from 8:00 a.m. to 8:00 p.m. Monday through Friday and has an answering service after hours and on weekends.

COST

Gateway is free.

STRENGTHS AND WEAKNESSES FOR USERS

The product allows one-stop access to the research activities of the U.S. government.

USER BASE

Not available.

USER SUPPORT

	N/A	Available	Comments
Consultants	x		
Documentation	x		
Training Classes	x		
Telephone Support		x	

VENDOR CONTACT

National Technology Transfer Center (NTTC)
Wheeling Jesuit College
316 Washington Avenue
Wheeling, WV 26003
Customer service representatives are available by calling (800) 678-6882.

HANDBOOK OF DESIGN AND PRODUCTION— ROLL FORMING

DESCRIPTION

The Handbook of Design and Production—Roll Forming describes the roll forming process, its advantages, equipment used in the process, and its history. It also discusses basic design tips and recent industry trends and provides a list of common materials roll formed, applications for roll-formed products, and tolerance guidelines. It concludes with a section titled "Designing for Economy."

HOW DO I USE IT?

This 12-page handbook originally appeared as a magazine article. It includes basic design tips, a list of common materials roll formed, applications for roll-formed products, tolerance guidelines, and a discussion of recent industry trends.

Cost

The *Handbook of Design and Production—Roll Forming* is available to PMA members for $2 and to non-members for $4.

Strengths and Weaknesses for Users

The handbook is brief and easy-to-read. It is not a comprehensive handbook by any means and should be used as an overview. It is extremely affordable.

User Base

The Precision Metalforming Association (PMA) represents the $31 billion metalforming industry of North America. Its more than 1,300 member companies include metal stampers, fabricators, spinners, and roll formers, as well as suppliers of equipment, materials, and services to the industry.

User Support

	N/A	Available	Comments
Consultants	x		
Documentation	x		
Training Classes	x		
Telephone Support	x		

Vendor Contact

PMA
27027 Chardon Road
Richmond Heights, Ohio 44143
VOICE   (216) 585-8800
FAX   (216) 585-3126

HANDSNET

Description

HandsNet is a privately operated, nonprofit computer network which links organizations working on a broad range of human-services issues. Unlike other on-line services, *HandsNet's* goal is to enhance and promote collaboration and cross-sector learning throughout the human services community. *HandsNet's* public forums cover such issues as health reform, hunger and nutrition policy, drug and substance abuse, housing and community development, legal services, rural poverty and development, children, youth and families, AIDS and HIV, the federal budget, and state and national policy.

How Do I Use It?

The user may access *HandsNet* by accessing the service from a Macintosh, Windows, or MS-DOS environment with a modem. *HandsNet* supports 1,200 bps to 14,400 bps modems.

Cost

Access to *HandsNet* is available for $150 per year for grassroots group membership and $270 per year for regular membership.

Strengths and Weaknesses for Users

Advantages to *HandsNet* include:

- access to a great deal of information;
- ability to conduct keyword searches; and
- contact with leaders in the field of human services.

User Base

HandsNet has been accessed by thousands of members.

User Support

	N/A	Available	Comments
Consultants	x		
Documentation		x	
Training Classes		x	
Telephone Support		x	

Vendor Contact

Sam Karp, Executive Director
HandsNet
20195 Stevens Creek Blvd., Suite 120
Cupertino, CA 95014
VOICE   (408) 257-4500
FAX   (408) 257-4560
E-MAIL   HN0012@handsnet.org

How to Stay on Top of Bar Codes

Description

How to Stay on Top of Bar Codes is a detailed yet easy-to-understand guide that examines the growing trends and technologies associated with bar codes. Information found in the updated, 20-page booklet includes the benefits of bar coding, terminology, bar code types, facts concerning the latest printing technologies, and more.

How Do I Use It?

How to Stay on Top of Bar Codes can be used as a handy pocket reference guide. The guide offers information about bar code types such as Universal Product Code or UPC, Interleaved 2-of-5, Code 39, Code 128, and PDF417.

Cost

How to Stay on Top of Bar Codes is available free of charge.

Strengths and Weaknesses for Users

The short booklet is just that—a short booklet. It does not offer detailed information. However, it does include handy reference material such as the bar code terminology section. The booklet's free availability is a plus.

User Base

Weber has been simplifying product identification, inventory control, material handling and other labeling problems for over 60 years. Weber has combined its labeling knowledge with over 15 years of bar coding experience and the latest bar code printing technology to provide the user with complete labeling solutions.

User Support

	N/A	Available	Comments
Consultants	x		
Documentation	x		
Training Classes	x		
Telephone Support	x		

Vendor Contact

Weber Marketing Systems, Inc.
711 W. Algonquin Road
Arlington Heights, IL 60005-4457
VOICE   (708) 364-8500
FAX   (708) 364-8575

INDUSTRY CONNECT ™

Description

Industry Connect™ is a new on-line information service developed by the National Center for Manufacturing Sciences (NCMS). In addition to a substantial public access section, the service provides NCMS members with an opportunity to access manufacturing information, perform literature searches, conduct research, and promote their products and services on the Internet.

How Do I Use It?

Industry Connect™ is available only through the Internet. For best access, the user should have a graphical internet browser such as Mosaic© or Netscape©. The Internet address for *Industry Connect™* is: *http://www.ncms.org.*

Cost

The public has free access to large portions of *Industry Connect™*. These portions do not include the on-line information service. NCMS members have unlimited access to *Industry Connect™* services. NCMS has created a special class of membership (Associate Membership) for companies who are interested in information access only at NCMS. The annual fee for this category of membership is $2,000 per year, regardless of company size. Associate Membership provides two accounts with unlimited access plus other advantages.

Strengths and Weaknesses for Users

Internet access is required. NCMS has established a world-class industrial R&D database, with topics ranging from plasma spray coating technologies to management issues.

User Base

There are more than 800 members' *Industry Connect™* accounts active today.

User Support

	N/A	Available	Comments
Consultants	x		
Documentation		x	Available on-line to public training integrated with on-line service.
Training Classes	x		
Telephone Support		x	

Vendor Contact

National Center for Manufacturing Sciences
3025 Boardwalk
Ann Arbor, MI 48108-3266
Industry Connect™: Carol Asquith (313) 995-3236
Membership: Dick Macan   (313) 995-7985

INTERNATIONAL TECHNOLOGY & BUSINESS OPPORTUNITIES DATABASE

DESCRIPTION

International Technology & Business Opportunities (ITBO) Database, a product of Klenner International, Inc., is a database service available worldwide. Formerly Dr. Dvorkovitz & Associates, Klenner International, Inc. has been in the business of technology transfer for 32 years. They pioneered on-line search-and-retrieval more than three decades ago and continue to be a global leader through their network of over 2,000 worldwide sources. With more than 30,000 technologies listed in 56 technical categories, Klenner International, Inc. has been involved in the licensing of more than 1,000 products and processes throughout the world.

HOW DO I USE IT?

Sources of new technology and business opportunities may be listed in the *ITBO Database* at no charge. Klenner International, Inc., provides this service to encourage global technology transfer. The organization offers a number of standard subscription services to organizations who are looking for new technologies from outside sources. Klenner International, Inc., also offers a full database of technologies in software format to organizations around the world for exclusive use in specific territories.

COST

Costs range from $200 for single searches to annual retrainers of $1,995 for specific categories. A standard subscription service which allows searches for up to 10 categories of technology is available for $1,000 annually and $50 per abstract.

STRENGTHS AND WEAKNESSES FOR USERS

ITBO is an international database. Klenner International, Inc. is currently working on establishing "franchise" databases in both Europe and Asia. These franchises bring in technologies from their territories to the main database in Ormond Beach, Florida. Information is then redistributed to other franchises and clients throughout the world. Some database services, such as subscribing annually to the specific search service, may be cost-prohibitive for individuals and smaller companies.

USER BASE

Klenner International, Inc. serves large corporations throughout the world by locating new opportunities for them. The company also serves government agencies, universities, research institutions, and large and small companies by finding licenses for their developments. Selected individuals also use the *ITBO Database* for listing their technologies.

USER SUPPORT

	N/A	Available	Comments
Consultants		x	
Documentation		x	
Training Classes	x		
Telephone Support	x		

VENDOR CONTACT

Anne E. Klenner
Klenner International, Inc.
P.O. Box 1748
Ormond Beach, FL 32175
VOICE   (904) 673-4339
FAX   (904) 673-5911

INVENTION NOTEBOOK RESOURCES

DESCRIPTION

Invention Notebook Resources is a 12-page pamphlet that explains the effects of NAFTA and GATT on U.S. Patent Law and provides step-by-step instructions about how to establish lab notebook procedures to create legal evidence to prove a date of invention.

HOW DO I USE IT?

The pamphlet is intended to be a step-by-step instruction guide on how to establish laboratory notebook procedures.

COST

The pamphlet is free to companies that do research and development.

STRENGTHS AND WEAKNESSES FOR USERS

The pamphlet is written by a practicing U.S. patent attorney (with American and foreign clients) who is familiar with patent prosecution and litigation under the new statutes.

The *Invention Notebook Procedures* pamphlet has been provided to all Morrison Law Firm clients and prospective clients. It has been in demand both here and abroad.

USER BASE

Any business or manufacturer engaged in research and development.

USER SUPPORT

	N/A	Available	Comments
Consultants		x	
Documentation	x		
Training Classes	x		
Telephone Support		x	

VENDOR CONTACT

Frank Nardozzi, Director
Marketing and Community Relations
Morrison Law Firm
145 North Fifth Avenue
Mount Vernon, NY 10550
VOICE   (914) 667-6755
FAX   (914) 667-7178

KNOWLEDGE EXPRESS DATA SYSTEMS

DESCRIPTION

Knowledge Express, a product of Knowledge Express Data Systems, is an on-line database service which provides information about corporate, university, and federal technology transfer opportunities, licensing opportunities, and collaborative ventures. The service offers access to more than 20 databases, including federal technologies and inventions (including DoD, DOE, NASA, PHS, EPA, NIST, USDA/ARS), Bioscan, Comtex Business News, Corptech, Technology Express News, NASA Tech Briefs, MicroPatent Alert, as well as the unique KEDS Company and Universities Technologies databases and Company Needs and Capabilities database.

In addition to a proprietary database service, *Knowledge Express* also offers its customers a full range of Internet services, including home page design and hosting along with World Wide Web marketing opportunities. By providing technical and R&D oriented companies with a comprehensive on-line search capability bundled with extensive on-line promotional and marketing opportunities, *Knowledge Express* delivers business development options and technology commercialization for today and tomorrow.

HOW DO I USE IT?

Knowledge Express can be used with either an IBM personal computer or compatible, Apple Macintosh, or Power PC computer. Users may employ traditional database searching techniques or may use Knowledge Express Data System's own search system, which allows advanced sorting and searching methods. Full Internet functionality will be available by the end of November, 1995.

COST

Knowledge Express is available for three monthly pricing packages from $49.95 to $189.95 per month. Pricing options may allow the user unlimited use of particular databases and a pre-determined amount of connect time. Government sponsored discounts are available for small to mid-sized companies with less than 500 employees.

STRENGTHS AND WEAKNESSES FOR USERS

The product's strengths are its:

- capacity to both search for and list technologies under development;
- easy, intuitive search interface and front end; and
- flexible pricing, with discounts to small and medium-sized companies.

USER BASE

Knowledge Express has more than 2,000 subscribers.

USER SUPPORT

	N/A	Available	Comments
Consultants		x	Three full-time Information Specialists
Documentation		x	*Knowledge Express* comes with a 32-page user's guide.
Training Classes		x	Phone training, user groups at seminars, conferences, etc.
Telephone Support	x		

VENDOR CONTACT

Knowledge Express Data Systems
1235 Weslakes Drive, Suite 210
Berwyn, PA 19312
Attn: Scott Gamble
Manager of Marketing & Sales
VOICE   (800) 529-5337
                (610) 251-0190
FAX   (610) 251-8001
E-MAIL   gamble@keds.com

MANUFACTURING ASSESSMENT METHODOLOGY

DESCRIPTION

The *Manufacturing Assessment Methodology (MAM)*, offered by the Michigan Manufacturing Technology Center (MMTC), is a systematic method for reviewing a company's manufacturing operation using a structured 14-step process. It is designed to examine parts of a manufacturing plant, help the company articulate its goals, and make recommendations for improvement. The output of this process is a 20- to 50-page final report and a half-day presentation to the client firm that summarizes the recommendations and lays out the action play for recommended improvement projects. The focus areas include: manufacturing processes; equipment/technology; scheduling and material control; estimating and planning systems; sales and marketing; management and organization; and training and education.

How Do I Use It?

MAM is used by a team of two to three field engineers who have a strong background in manufacturing or small business practices and have attended the MMTC'S three-day *MAM* training workshop. The *MAM* team gathers preliminary data about the company using the appropriate MMTC Performance Benchmarking questionnaire and by conducting phone interviews. The team conducts the actual site assessment, which includes confirming questionnaire responses, observing operations, conducting interviews, and reviewing documents—all with the aid of the *MAM* Tool Kit of checklists and guidelines. The team analyzes the data collected and presents their preliminary findings to the firm. Firm personnel provide confirmation and further data, and they prioritize their goals with the team's help. Afterward, the team further examines the data and writes a final report with recommendations for four or five projects. The process ends with the team presenting their findings to the client firm and assisting with implementation of selected projects.

Cost

MMTC charges firms $6,000 to $8,000 for each *MAM*. The cost for the *MAM* three-day training is $1,200 per person at the MMTC location in Ann Arbor, Michigan; the cost includes materials, meals, and the *MAM* license. MMTC recommends that trainees work with experienced *MAM* users on several assessments before taking the lead on their own. MMTC will travel to provide training for up to 18 participants for $16,000 plus travel expense. For additional fees, trainers also will travel to assist trainees with initial assessments.

Strengths and Weaknesses for Users

MAM is a structured, well-documented methodology that anyone with a manufacturing or small business background can follow. The documentation includes a process manual and a rich, in-depth Tool Kit containing guidelines and tools for data gathering and analysis. *MAM* is a comprehensive, third-party data collection tool; it allows client interaction throughout the process that assists in client "buy-in" and delivers results and projects that are tailored to the individual client. *MAM* sales are challenged by the high cost relative to self-assessments and questionnaires, its difficulty in selling value (benefits versus costs), and by the fact that it is not effective for an agency to use as a conversation starter or wake-up call.

User Base

Since 1991, *MAM* has been used to assess more than 80 companies. While it can be used to assist all types of manufacturing firms of any size, it is most often used with firms of 20 to 400 workers. MMTC's primary industry sectors include metalforming, tooling and machining, and plastics. *MAM* and *MAM*-based assessment tools are used by MMTC, California Manufacturing Technology

Center, Alberta (Canada) Research Council, State of Maine, Air Force Programs, Department of Energy, Institute for Advanced Manufacturing Sciences (Ohio), Edison Welding Institute, and private consultants.

USER SUPPORT

	N/A	Available	Comments
Consultants		x	Lead assessors or assessments available at $725 per person per day. Production staff available at $400 per day.
Documentation		x	Three-manual set available for $400.
Training Classes		x	Three-day workshop at $1,200 per person or $15,000 plus travel for off-site, up to 20 participants.
Telephone Support		x	During the course of the assessment and one month after training.

VENDOR CONTACT

Dave Arnsdorf
MMTC
2901 Hubbard Rd.
Ann Arbor, MI 48105
VOICE   (313) 769-4178
FAX   (313) 769-4064
E-MAIL   dra@iti.org

D. Ortiz, Programs Manager, *MAM* Training
MMTC
2901 Hubbard Rd.
Ann Arbor, MI 48105
(313) 769-4107
(313) 769-4064
dlo@iti.org

MAM training:
Joan Carvell, Deputy Director
California Manufacturing Technology Center
VOICE   (310) 355-3060

All engineer/technologists hired by the CMTC must attend the MMTC's *MAM* three-day workshop.

MANUFACTURING INFORMATION RESOURCE CENTER— RESEARCH SERVICES AND LIBRARY RESOURCES

DESCRIPTION

The *Manufacturing Information Resource Center (MIRC)* is a service of the National Center for Manufacturing Sciences. *MIRC* provides rapid, accurate solutions to manufacturing problems. It consists of a Research Services group and a 40,000-volume collection devoted solely to manufacturing technology and management practices. The Research Services staff are expert in using a myriad of external business and scientific databases to address manufacturing R&D issues. The collection is made up of books, technical reports, journals, videotapes, audiocassettes, market research studies, and more.

How Do I Use It?

MIRC is a service to NCMS members. Members access *MIRC* either by phone request or on-line search of the Library Catalog (see *Industry Connect*™). NCMS membership is available to North American-owned entities committed to improving manufacturing competitiveness in the U.S., Canada, and Mexico.

Cost

Active Membership dues in NCMS are on a graduated scale according to annual sales. Smaller companies (up to $20M sales) pay $2,000 per year in dues. This provides a wide range of benefits including full access to *MIRC*.

Strengths and Weaknesses for Users

MIRC represents a comprehensive resource of materials dedicated to manufacturing.

User Base

There are more than 200 members of NCMS who use *MIRC* at a very high rate.

User Support

	N/A	Available	Comments
Consultants		x	Expert research staff.
Documentation		x	
Training Classes	x		
Telephone Support		x	

Vendor Contact

National Center for Manufacturing Sciences
3025 Boardwalk
Ann Arbor, MI 48108-3266
MIRC: Kate Brayton   (313) 995-3095
Membership: Dick Macan   (313) 995-7985

MANUALLY FED PRESS OPERATOR AND DIE SETTER TRAINING

DESCRIPTION

This tool is a video training system produced by the Precision Metalforming Association (PMA). It teaches press operators and die setters the basics of manually fed press operation. Topics include: basic machine components, safe operation, die components and operation, indicators of incorrect operation, measuring and gauging piece parts, setup controls and tools, installing die assembly, and trial stamping the first piece part.

HOW DO I USE IT?

The system includes easy-to-follow instructions, eight VHS videotapes, an operator manual, a manager manual, a supervisor manual, a grader manual, five written job aides to provide additional information and supporting materials too complex for the videotapes, and completion certificates.

COST

The cost is $2,400 for PMA members for the first set and $400 for each additional set. The cost for non-PMA members is $4,800 for each set. There is a $15 shipping cost per set.

STRENGTHS AND WEAKNESSES FOR USERS

This tool provides needed training for new employees and refresher courses for others. It requires full management backing and participation.

USER BASE

The Precision Metalforming Association (PMA) represents the $31 billion metalforming industry of North America. Its more than 1,300 member companies include metal stampers, fabricators, spinners, and roll formers, as well as suppliers of equipment, materials, and services to the industry.

USER SUPPORT

	N/A	Available	Comments
Consultants	x		
Documentation	x		
Training Classes	x		
Telephone Support	x		

VENDOR CONTACT

PMA
27027 Chardon Road
Richmond Heights, Ohio 44143
VOICE   (216) 585-8800
FAX   (216) 585-3126

Metal Spinning Machine Operator Training

Description

This tool is a video training system produced by the Precision Metalforming Association (PMA). It teaches employees the basic operation of automatic metal spinning machines. The system can be used as safety training for hand spinners and other shop employees or for general education purposes.

How Do I Use It?

The system includes easy-to-follow instructions, two VHS videotapes, an operator manual, a manager manual, a supervisor manual, lesson worksheets, performance tests, and completion certificates.

Cost

The cost is $1,000 for PMA members for the first set and $300 for each additional set. The cost for non-PMA members is $2,000 for the first set and $600 for each additional set.

Strengths and Weaknesses for Users

This tool provides needed training for new employees and refresher courses for others. It requires full management backing and participation.

User Base

The Precision Metalforming Association (PMA) represents the $31 billion metalforming industry of North America. Its more than 1,300 member companies include metal stampers, fabricators, spinners, and roll formers, as well as suppliers of equipment, materials, and services to the industry.

User Support

	N/A	Available	Comments
Consultants	x		
Documentation	x		
Training Classes	x		
Telephone Support	x		

Vendor Contact

PMA
27027 Chardon Road
Richmond Heights, Ohio 44143
VOICE   (216) 585-8800
FAX   (216) 585-3126

MICROPATENT

DESCRIPTION

MicroPatent offers CD-ROM products to perform patent and trademark searches without the high cost of more traditional methods. CDs containing entire patent documents, including drawings, are also available for companies which have a need for large quantities of patent documents. *MicroPatent* also offers custom products to meet individual user's specifications regarding contents and features needed. When the need for patent searches or patent copies is only occasional, *MicroPatent's* PatentQuery Division will provide the answers. Call them to request patent searches or patent copies at very reasonable prices.

MicroPatent even offers patent searching and document delivery via the Internet. Search the last two weeks of U.S. patents or view the front pages of any U.S. patent since 1975, free of charge. Download patents immediately for only 25¢ per page. One may order patent copies that are delivered by fax or mail. Be sure to visit the company's home page on the World Wide Web at *http://www.micropat.com.*

HOW DO I USE IT?

MicroPatent's CD-ROM products are available for use on DOS-based IBM compatible computers. Some products have Windows versions available, and custom products are available on a variety of platforms including Lotus Notes. All *MicroPatent* products are designed to be simple to use, yet powerful enough to handle the most demanding search strategies.

If one prefers to have searches performed by one of *MicroPatent's* professional patent searchers, they can be reached directly at (800) 984-9800. Patent copies can also be ordered at that number.

COST

MicroPatent offers CD-ROM products to match almost any need and budget with prices starting at $295. PatentQuery's search services range from approximately $30 for simple short-range searches to around $250 for the most comprehensive searches.

STRENGTHS AND WEAKNESSES FOR USERS

MicroPatent's greatest strengths lie in the diversity of products, their simplicity, and their full range of features. Products and services are available for any budget or need. Although most products are designed for use on IBM compatible computers, there are other options currently available and still more being developed.

USER BASE

MicroPatent's clients include:

Corporate Libraries	Marketing Managers
Legal Departments	Patent Attorneys
Government Researchers	Individual Inventors
R&D Departments	Engineers

USER SUPPORT

	N/A	Available	Comments
Consultants		x	
Documentation		x	
Training Classes		x	On-site at customer premises.
Telephone Support		x	M-F 8:30 to 5:00 ET.

VENDOR CONTACT

MicroPatent
250 Dodge Avenue
East Haven, CT 06512-3358
VOICE   (800) 984-9800
         (203) 466-5055
FAX   (203) 466-5054
E-MAIL   info@micropat.com

MORRISON LAW FIRM NEWSLETTER

DESCRIPTION

The *Morrison Law Firm Newsletter* is published periodically by the Morrison Patent Law Firm of Mount Vernon, New York. The *Newsletter* deals with subjects pertaining to patents, copyrights, and trademarks and seeks to illuminate current topics of interest such as GATT and "Submarine Patents."

HOW DO I USE IT?

The *Newsletter* is for general information and usually offers a point of view about developments of concern to companies who possess intellectual property.

COST

Newsletters are provided free of charge to companies who possess patents, copyrights, or trademarks or are interested in developing their intellectual property.

STRENGTHS AND WEAKNESSES FOR USERS

The *Newsletter* provides the insight of an international patent attorney into developments affecting intellectual property. The *Newsletter* goes beyond providing information to analyzing the effects that new developments may have. Companies with intellectual property (patents, copyrights, or trademarks) have found the *Newsletter* outspoken, useful, and informative.

USER BASE

Companies who possess or have an interest in developing patents, copyrights, and trademarks.

USER SUPPORT

	N/A	Available	Comments
Consultants		x	
Documentation	x		
Training Classes	x		
Telephone Support		x	

VENDOR CONTACT

Frank Nardozzi, Director
Marketing and Community Relations
Morrison Law Firm
145 North Fifth Avenue
Mount Vernon, NY 10550
VOICE   (914) 667-6755
FAX   (914) 667-7178

PATENT AND TRADEMARK DEPOSITORY LIBRARY (PTDL) PROGRAM NETWORK

DESCRIPTION

The *PTDL Program* is a growing network of 78 academic, public, state, and special research libraries in 49 states, the District of Columbia, and Puerto Rico working in partnership with the U.S. Patent and Trademark Office (USPTO) to disseminate intellectual property to the nation. These libraries maintain collections of full-text U.S. patents, trademark records, the *Official Gazette*, and various indexing and search tools in a variety of formats. The collections are available for use by the public in performing searches prior to filing applications and are updated weekly as patents and trademarks are issued. Some of the libraries also maintain varying sizes of foreign patent collections.

HOW DO I USE IT?

Trained staff at the *PTDL* will assist public users in accessing the collections, but will not conduct patent or trademark searches for patrons. The U.S. patents are filed in numerical order by patent number. Various tools index patent and trademark information by subject matter, classification and inventor or owner name to facilitate use of the collection. CD-ROM search tools containing patent and trademark information are available at each library. To further assist with patent searching, many *PTDLs* offer access to the Automated Patent System (APS), an on-line database containing full-text U.S. patents dating from 1971.

COST

The use of *PTDL* depository collections is free. Charges for photocopies, prints from computers, or Interlibrary Loan Services vary by library. Fees for use of the APS vary by library.

STRENGTHS AND WEAKNESSES FOR USERS

PTDL staff may not render legal opinions on intellectual property matters (defined broadly). Backfiles of patent collections vary by library. The minimum backfile is 20 years, but many maintain complete collections dating from 1790. The APS database is available only at subscribing *PTDLs*. Foreign patent collections vary by library. A wider variety of services is available at the *PTDLs* in Sunnyvale, CA and Detroit, MI. These *PTDLs* have entered into cost-sharing agreements with the USPTO to offer the APS, patent images on-line, videoconferencing between patent examiners and inventors or attorneys, more in-depth seminars and, soon, on-line trademark searching.

PTDLs maintain directories for referral purposes, participate in or keep files on young inventor programs, cooperate with inventor organizations (*not* invention marketing firms) and enjoy an active liaison with the USPTO to be current on all pending and recent legislation or procedural changes.

USER BASE

PTDL users are made up of entrepreneurs, inventors, researchers, information brokers, intellectual property attorneys, faculty, students, historians and those associated with small business start-up activities.

USER SUPPORT

	N/A	Available	Comments
Consultants		x	*PTDL* staff assist users.
Documentation	x		
Training Classes	x		
Telephone Support		x	

VENDOR CONTACT

Martha Crockett Sneed
Patent and Trademark Depository Library Program
U.S. Patent and Trademark Office
Crystal Plaza 3, Suite 481
Washington, DC 20231
VOICE   (703) 308-5558
FAX   (703) 306-2654

PLASTICS ENGINEERING HANDBOOK

DESCRIPTION

This handbook offers detailed information on plastics—chemistry, applications, processing, machinery and more—in a single convenient reference. The handbook gives real-life instruction on polymer chemistry, materials application and properties and processing methods. It covers the entire cycle of the design and manufacture of plastic products including materials selection, parts design, process technology, finishing work, testing and troubleshooting.

HOW DO I USE IT?

An extensive table of contents and a comprehensive index allow for easy identification of needed information.

COST

Members of the Society of the Plastics Industry, $69.95; non-members, $79.95.

STRENGTHS AND WEAKNESSES FOR USERS

The handbook gives pragmatic instruction in a comprehensive list of engineering issues in the plastics industry.

USER BASE

Not available.

USER SUPPORT

	N/A	Available	Comments
Consultants	x		
Documentation		x	
Training Classes	x		
Telephone Support	x		

VENDOR CONTACT

The Society of the Plastics Industry, Inc.
1275 K Street, NW, #400
Washington, DC 20005-4006
VOICE   (202) 371-5257

PMA DESIGN GUIDELINES FOR METAL STAMPINGS AND FABRICATIONS (2ND EDITION)

DESCRIPTION

PMA Design Guidelines for Metal Stampings and Fabrications highlights key design issues that arise most frequently when working with metal stamping and fabricated metal parts. It features design information and provides practical, cost-effective solutions. The guide provides valuable assistance on the factory floor, the drawing board, or at the CAD terminal. New chapters on spinning and rollforming now includes CAD guidelines.

HOW DO I USE IT?

The guide is organized for easy reference and includes illustrations, tables, and a glossary of 400 common terms to help provide easy comprehension.

COST

A single copy of *PMA Design Guidelines for Metal Stampings and Fabrications* is available to PMA members for $39.95 and to non-members for $69.95, plus $4.50 shipping per book. Discounts are available when purchasing multiple copies. Members purchasing 50 or more copies can arrange to have the cover of their manuals imprinted with the message, "Compliments of (company name)."

STRENGTHS AND WEAKNESSES FOR USERS

The manual is a valuable and authoritative resource published for those who specify, design, and purchase stamped and fabricated metal parts and assemblies. It is a good primer for the inexperienced designer as well as a reference for the accomplished professional.

USER BASE

The Precision Metalforming Association (PMA) represents the $31 billion metalforming industry of North America. Its more than 1,200 member companies include metal stampers, fabricators, spinners, and roll formers, as well as suppliers of equipment, materials, and services to the industry.

USER SUPPORT

	N/A	Available	Comments
Consultants	x		
Documentation	x		
Training Classes	x		
Telephone Support	x		

VENDOR CONTACT

PMA
27027 Chardon Road
Richmond Heights, Ohio 44143
VOICE   (216) 585-8800
FAX   (216) 585-3126

PMWS (PROGRAM MANAGER'S WORKSTATION)

DESCRIPTION

The *Program Manager's Workstation* (PMWS) is a suite of tools designed to help a program manager guide his or her development program through the complicated systems engineering process of design, development, and production. The workstation currently consists of four tools which are described in detail in this catalog individually: *SpecRite, KnowHow, TRIMS*, and the *BMP Database*.

SpecRite is an automated performance specification generator. *KnowHow* is an electronic library on systems engineering which contains several expert systems on system development. *TRIMS* is a technical risk identification and mitigation system; *TRIMS* enables a manager to avoid risks inherent in system development by identifying them early in the program, before they develop cost and schedule overruns. The *BMP Database* hosts current best practices from industry primarily in the manufacturing arena.

How Do I Use It?

Users can access this software via *BMPnet*, a Navy-sponsored dial-up network. The tool can be used while connected, or it can be downloaded to any DOS-based personal computer. The full PMWS requires about 80 megabytes of disk space.

Cost

Free to industry and government personnel (continental U.S. only).

Strengths and Weaknesses for Users

PMWS is based on the Critical Path Templates, providing a comprehensive framework for systems engineering.

User Base

Current user base is represented by the annual call volume on *BMPnet,* recently over 70,000 calls per year.

User Support

	N/A	Available	Comments
Consultants		x	
Documentation		x	
Training Classes		x	
Telephone Support		x	

Vendor Contact

BMP COE
4321 Hartwick Road, Suite 308
College Park, MD 20740
VOICE   (301) 403-8100
FAX   (301) 403-8180
BMPnet   (703) 538-7697
BMP Help Desk (703) 538-7253
E-MAIL   bmpinfo@bmpcoe.org
URL   http://www.bmpcoe.org

PMWS: BMP DATABASE

DESCRIPTION

The *BMP Database*, part of the Program Manager's Workstation (PMWS), is a database which hosts abstracts of best practices from American companies and government labs/centers on manufacturing and engineering.

HOW DO I USE IT?

Users can access this software via *BMPnet*, a Navy-sponsored dial-up network. The tool can be used while connected, or it can be downloaded to any DOS-based personal computer. To use the database, users simply follow on-screen prompts to browse abstracts, search, and create reports. To access *BMPnet*, call the HelpDesk below, or dial the BMP number below, and follow on-screen instructions for downloading the ONLAN software, which is the preferred communications package for use with *BMPnet*.

COST

Free to industry and government personnel (continental U.S. only).

STRENGTHS AND WEAKNESSES FOR USERS

PMWS is based on the Critical Path Templates, providing a comprehensive framework for systems engineering.

USER BASE

Current user base is represented by call volume on *BMPnet*: over 70,000 calls per year.

USER SUPPORT

	N/A	Available	Comments
Consultants		x	
Documentation		x	
Training Classes		x	
Telephone Support		x	

VENDOR CONTACT

BMP COE
4321 Hartwick Road, Suite 308
College Park, MD 20740
VOICE   (301) 403-8100
FAX   (301) 403-8180
BMPnet   (703) 538-7697
BMP Help Desk (703) 538-7253
E-MAIL   bmpinfo@bmpcoe.org
URL   http://www.bmpcoe.org

PMWS: KNOWHOW

DESCRIPTION

KnowHow, part of the Program Manager's Workstation (PMWS), is an electronic library of full-text resources in the realm of systems engineering. The main expert system in this library contains a systems engineering task model that guides users in every phase of product development. Users need only follow simple menus and answer questions to arrive at pertinent information on the task they are facing within systems engineering (i.e. trade-off-studies, requirements allocation, integrated test plan, etc.) The information is based on the Critical Path Template, "How to Avoid Surprises in the Transition from Development to Production," DoD 4245.7-M.

HOW DO I USE IT?

Users can access this software via *BMPnet*, a Navy-sponsored dial-up network. The tool can be used while connected, or it can be downloaded to any DOS-based personal computer. To use *KnowHow* itself, users simply browse the menu hierarchy. Search and print functions are available as well.

COST

Free to industry and government personnel (contintental U.S. only).

STRENGTHS AND WEAKNESSES FOR USERS

PMWS is based on the Critical Path Templates, providing a comprehensive framework for systems engineering.

USER BASE

Current user base is represented by the annual call volume on *BMPnet*, recently over 70,000 calls per year.

USER SUPPORT

	N/A	Available	Comments
Consultants		x	
Documentation		x	
Training Classes		x	
Telephone Support		x	

VENDOR CONTACT

BMP COE
4321 Hartwick Road, Suite 308
College Park, MD 20740
VOICE   (301) 403-8100
FAX   (301) 403-8180
BMPnet   (703) 538-7697
BMP Help Desk (703) 538-7253
E-MAIL   bmpinfo@bmpcoe.org
URL   http://www.bmpcoe.org

PMWS: SpecRite

DESCRIPTION

SpecRite, part of the Program Manager's Workstation, is a performance specification generator. *SpecRite* guides the user in determining interface and environmental (temperature, vibration, etc.) requirements, and provides features for managing the specification/requirements build process. *SpecRite* uses standard formats including the use of WordPerfect DOS 5.1 format, and MIL-STD-961D.

HOW DO I USE IT?

Users can access this software via *BMPnet*, a Navy-sponsored dial-up network. The tool can be used while connected, or it can be downloaded to any DOS-based personal computer. To use *SpecRite* itself, users create a *SpecRite* file and then proceed through Build Spec and Review Edit functions to develop their performance spec.

COST

Free to industry and government personnel (continental U.S. only).

STRENGTHS AND WEAKNESSES FOR USERS

PMWS is based on the Critical Path Templates, providing a comprehensive framework for systems engineering.

USER BASE

Current user base is represented by call volume on *BMPnet*: over 70,000 calls per year.

USER SUPPORT

	N/A	Available	Comments
Consultants		x	
Documentation		x	
Training Classes		x	
Telephone Support		x	

VENDOR CONTACT

BMP COE
4321 Hartwick Road, Suite 308
College Park, MD 20740
VOICE   (301) 403-8100
FAX   (301) 403-8180
BMPnet   (703) 538-7697
BMP Help Desk (703) 538-7253
E-MAIL   bmpinfo@bmpcoe.org
URL   http://www.bmpcoe.org

PMWS: TRIMS

DESCRIPTION

TRIMS, part of the Program Manager's Workstation, is a technical risk identification and mitigation system. *TRIMS* enables a manager to avoid risks inherent in system development by identifying them early in the program, before they develop cost and schedule overruns. The information in *TRIMS* is based on the Template, "How to Avoid Surprises in the Transition from Development to Production." The system qualifies disciplines within systems engineering with respect to risk as Red, Yellow, or Green (i.e. Trade-off Studies under Design is Yellow) based on compliance with its internal knowledge of the systems engineering process.

HOW DO I USE IT?

Users can access this software via *BMPnet*, a Navy-sponsored dial-up network. The tool can be used while connected, or it can be downloaded to any DOS-based personal computer. To use *TRIMS* itself, users should plan on spending a considerable effort in gathering systems documentation.

COST

Free to industry and government personnel (continental U.S. only).

STRENGTHS AND WEAKNESSES FOR USERS

PMWS is based on the Critical Path Templates, providing a comprehensive framework for systems engineering.

USER BASE

Current user base is represented by the annual call volume on *BMPnet*, recently over 70,000 calls per year.

USER SUPPORT

	N/A	Available	Comments
Consultants		x	
Documentation		x	
Training Classes		x	
Telephone Support		x	

VENDOR CONTACT

BMP COE
4321 Hartwick Road, Suite 308
College Park, MD 20740
VOICE   (301) 403-8100
FAX   (301) 403-8180
BMPnet   (703) 538-7697
BMP Help Desk (703) 538-7253
E-MAIL   bmpinfo@bmpcoe.org
URL   http://www.bmpcoe.org

POLLUTION PREVENTION RESEARCH PUBLICATIONS LISTING

DESCRIPTION

This listing describes nearly 200 publications that describe how to prevent pollution in specific industries. Industries covered in the listing include: mechanical equipment repair, metal casting and heat treating, metal finishing, machined tools and parts, and coatings. Publications are also available for preventing pollution in certain processes dealing with coatings, cleaning, and finishes.

HOW DO I USE IT?

Each publication gives detailed instructions.

COST

Many reports are free of charge.

STRENGTHS AND WEAKNESSES FOR USERS

N/A

USER BASE

Not available.

USER SUPPORT

	N/A	Available	Comments
Consultants	x		
Documentation	x		
Training Classes	x		
Telephone Support	x		

VENDOR CONTACT

CERI Publications Unit, USEPA
26 W. Martin Luther King Drive
Cincinnati, OH 45244
VOICE   (513) 569-7562

PRECISION SHEET METAL FABRICATING

DESCRIPTION

This booklet serves as a guide for users of precision sheet metal fabrications. It also provides customers with an overview of the metal fabricating industry. The booklet covers manufacturing processes and methods and features a guide to purchasing precision sheet metal fabrications.

HOW DO I USE IT?

Precision Sheet Metal Fabricating can be used as an overview of the industry and of specific processes. It is 10 pages long and written in an easily understood style.

COST

Precision Sheet Metal Fabricating is available for $3 to PMA members and $7 to non-members. Quantity discounts are available.

STRENGTHS AND WEAKNESSES FOR USERS

The booklet is written in an easy-to-follow style so it may be referenced by industry users and customers alike. The guide functions best as an overview; it is not a detailed, step-by-step process guide. It is quite inexpensive.

USER BASE

The Precision Metalforming Association (PMA) represents the $31 billion metalforming industry of North America. Its more than 1,300 member companies include metal stampers, fabricators, spinners, and roll formers, as well as suppliers of equipment, materials, and services to the industry.

USER SUPPORT

	N/A	Available	Comments
Consultants	x		
Documentation	x		
Training Classes	x		
Telephone Support	x		

VENDOR CONTACT

PMA
27027 Chardon Road
Richmond Heights, Ohio 44143
VOICE   (216) 585-8800
FAX   (216) 585-3126

RAW MATERIAL BAR CODE LABELING GUIDE

DESCRIPTION

For coatings manufacturers and raw material suppliers, this guide is a helpful industry tool that can significantly enhance inventory management and improve the speed and accuracy of account recording. It is also an excellent method of automating "cradle-to-grave" tracking of raw materials used in finished products.

How Do I Use It?

The guide is comprised of bar code labels that can stand alone or be linked with electronic data interchange (EDI). As a stand-alone label, manufacturers can automatically record receipt of items listed on work orders by scanning four recommended segments of the bar code label. When used with EDI, the bar code enables manufacturers to automatically record necessary accounts payable and inventory information by scanning a single symbol.

Cost

The product is available to non-members for $350.

Strengths and Weaknesses for Users

Designed for coatings manufacturers' use, the guide can also be used to help suppliers improve the efficiency and accuracy of their handling of raw materials.

User Base

NPCA is a voluntary, nonprofit trade association representing some 500 paint and coatings manufacturers, raw materials suppliers and distributors. Collectively, NPCA's membership produces approximately 75 percent of the total dollar-volume of paints and industrial coatings sold in the United States.

User Support

	N/A	Available	Comments
Consultants	x		
Documentation	x		
Training Classes	x		
Telephone Support		x	

Vendor Contact

National Paint and Coatings Association
1500 Rhode Island Avenue, NW
Washington, DC 20005
VOICE   (202) 462-6272
FAX   (202) 462-8549

Reengineering the Factory: A Primer for World-Class Manufacturing

Description

This book is a primer on world-class manufacturing methods for those who want to understand them at a conceptual level. It addresses the functions, contributions, and interrelationships of eight primary methods used in industry today.

How Do I Use It?

Reengineering the Factory: A Primer for World-Class Manufacturing contains the following sections: economic growth model; total quality management; Kaizen-continuous improvement; total quality control; process of management; self-managed teams; quality function deployment; design for manufacturing; automation; computer-integrated manufacturing; just-in-time; the management system; training; ISO 9000—1987; Malcolm Baldridge National Quality Award; and implementation strategy. The book offers overviews of key concepts, emphasizes eight world-class manufacturing methods, and includes 25 illustrations and tables.

Cost

Reengineering the Factory: A Primer for World-Class Manufacturing is available for $15 to ASQC members and $17 to non-members.

Strengths and Weaknesses for Users

The book serves well as a quick reference guide. It gives the big picture of world-class manufacturing. It also is useful to show the relationships between functions and contributions of world-class manufacturing performance. The book's price should make it available to nearly everyone.

User Base

The book is available through the American Society for Quality Control (ASQC). With more than 130,000 individual members and 900 sustaining members, ASQC is one of the largest and most diverse professional organizations dedicated to quality.

User Support

	N/A	Available	Comments
Consultants	x		
Documentation	x		
Training Classes	x		
Telephone Support	x		

Vendor Contact

ASQC
P.O. Box 3005

Milwaukee, WI 53201-3005
VOICE   (800) 248-1946
URL   http://www.asqc.org

STANDARDS AND PRACTICES OF PLASTIC MOLDERS

DESCRIPTION

This guide provides information for the successful design of molded plastic parts, including advice on threads, inserts, fillets and radii, plus mold tolerance specification sheets covering 27 plastic resins, in both English and Metric units. It also provides guidelines for commercial and administrative practices for conducting business. Topics include contractual obligations, production and handling of tooling, charges and costs, packing and shipping, and other areas.

HOW DO I USE IT?

This guide is divided into subject matter with easy-to-identify topics.

COST

Costs depend on quantity:

Quantity 1	$15 each for members of the Society of the Plastics Industry, $30 each for non-members.
Quantity 2-10	$10 each for members, $20 for non-members.
Quantity 11-plus	$8 each for members, $16 each for non-members.

STRENGTHS AND WEAKNESSES FOR USERS

This guide provides an in-depth analysis of standards and practices in one specific industry—the plastic molding industry. It is only of use to participants in that industry.

USER BASE

Not available.

USER SUPPORT

	N/A	Available	Comments
Consultants	x		
Documentation		x	
Training Classes	x		
Telephone Support	x		

VENDOR CONTACT

The Society of the Plastics Industry, Inc.
1275 K Street, N.W., #400

Washington, DC 20005-4006
VOICE   (202) 371-5257

Statistical Process Control

Description

Customers are asking metalforming firms to practice many of the modern business techniques sweeping American manufacturers. These techniques include zero defects philosophies, just-in-time (JIT) delivery, quality improvement programs, and especially, statistical process control (SPC). Statistical process control applies statistical methods to the quality control processes. This 24-page manual explains the following:

1. Definition and description of SPC;
2. The importance of SPC; and
3. How to implement it in a firm's operations.

How Do I Use It?

The book is a handy reference guide that explains the role SPC plays in quality and how to implement statistical methods to improve specification design and process control.

Cost

The manual costs $5 for members of the Precision Metalforming Association and $8 for the general public.

Strengths and Weaknesses for Users

The manual offers instruction on SPC as it specifically applies to metalforming firms. Consequently, employees in metalforming firms will receive instruction specifically designed for their needs.

User Base

The Precision Metalforming Association represents the $31 billion metalforming industry of North America—the industry that gives utility to sheet metal by shaping it using tooling machines. The membership consists of more than 1,300 companies including metal stampers, fabricators, spinners, and roll formers, as well as suppliers of equipment, materials, and services to the industry.

User Support

	N/A	Available	Comments
Consultants	x		
Documentation	x		
Training Classes	x		
Telephone Support	x		

VENDOR CONTACT

The Precision Metalforming Association
27027 Chardon Road
Richmond Heights, OH 44143
VOICE   (216) 585-8800
FAX   (216) 585-3126

TECHNICAL INSIGHTS ALERT®

DESCRIPTION

TECHNICAL INSIGHTS ALERT®, a product of Technical Insights, Inc., is a weekly electronic wire service reporting on significant technical advances with near-term commercial potential. Ten critical areas are covered: industrial R&D, high-tech materials, coatings technology, advanced manufacturing, industrial bioprocessing, sensor technology, genetic technology, electronics technology, chemical process and bio/med technology. *ALERT* provides a screened executive presentation of 65-70 developments each week.

HOW DO I USE IT?

Clients receive an ASCII file of technical advances that can be uploaded to their computer network system (e-mail is the most preferred method). The file is transmitted via Internet, CompuServe, or modem directly to the client's network. *ALERT* is also compatible with Lotus Notes. Clients then distribute the information broadly to any number of people in the company.

COST

The cost of *TECHNICAL INSIGHTS ALERT* depends on the number of services subscribed to and whether *ALERT* is bought for a single-use site or for use throughout the corporation. Prices vary from $2,200 to $44,700 annually. Based on the usage of current clients, *ALERT* can cost as little as $50 a year per individual user.

STRENGTHS AND WEAKNESSES FOR USERS

ALERT provides early notification of significant technical opportunities and competitive threats. It also identifies those advances most likely to create industries and markets of the future or to irrevocably change existing ones. *ALERT* saves time and money. Comprehensive yet selective, it has already sifted through thousands of developments to identify truly significant advances that pose meaningful opportunities. *ALERT* allows one to build an in-house database of important technology and experts in a company's particular field of activity.

USER BASE

The product has approximately 5,100 to 5,800 users.

USER SUPPORT

	N/A	Available	Comments
Consultants		x	
Documentation	x		
Training Classes		x	
Telephone Support		x	

VENDOR CONTACT

Technical Insights, Inc.
P.O. Box 1304
Fort Lee, NJ 07024
Attn: Lyn Schmidt
Director of Marketing
VOICE   (201) 568-4744
FAX   (201) 568-8247
E-MAIL   lyn@insights.com
CompuServe 73373,51

TECHNOLOGY TRANSFER CATALOG

DESCRIPTION

The *Technology Transfer Catalog*, or *T^2 Catalog*, is a tool which allows both Department of Defense (DoD) and non-DoD organizations—including state and local governments, industry, and educational institutions—to access information about U.S. Army Space & Strategic Defense Command (USASSDC) technologies such as artificial intelligence, lasers, and composite materials. The catalog was developed as a tool to foster the transfer of information about USASSDC to military and federal laboratories, as well as to small businesses.

The *Technology Transfer Catalog* provides a short description of each technology along with technical objectives, schedules, technology products/prototypes, potential technology transfer applications, and technical points of contact. Current contents include technology programs which are currently funded by the USASSDC and SBIR programs. Future revisions will include information on patents available for licensing and negotiated Cooperative Research and Development Agreements (CRDAs).

HOW DO I USE IT?

The *Technology Transfer Catalog* comes on a single self-contained diskette and is quite user-friendly. It is available in either DOS-based personal computer format (two Mb RAM and 2.5 Mb hard drive space required) or Macintosh format (four Mb RAM recommended, four Mb hard drive space required). Instructions are included.

COST

There is no charge for the *Technology Transfer Catalog*; however, it is only available to U.S. government agencies and their contractors.

STRENGTHS AND WEAKNESSES FOR USERS

The virtue of a powerful tool that allows access to USASSDC technologies and is available at no cost is easy to appreciate. The *Technology Transfer Catalog* has been very well received in demonstrations before small businesses and U.S. Army laboratories and may become the standard for the U.S. Army. This can be an extremely useful tool for technology transfer from the defense sector and could be particularly useful for small businesses. In fact, the catalog should be attractive to anyone interested in transferring available defense technologies. A drawback of the catalog is that distribution is limited to U.S. government agencies and their contractors.

USER BASE

This catalog has been widely disseminated throughout the military and defense industry.

USER SUPPORT

	N/A	Available	Comments
Consultants	x		
Documentation	x		
Training Classes	x		
Telephone Support	x		

VENDOR CONTACT

Russ Alexander
USASSDC
Attn: CSSD-PI
P.O. Box 1500
Huntsville, AL 35807-3801
VOICE (205) 955-4763
FAX (205) 955-3958
E-MAIL alexander@ssdch_usassdc.army.mil

TECnet

DESCRIPTION

The Technologies for Effective Cooperation Network, or *TECnet*, is a customized gateway which offers users interested in manufacturing a convenient way to tap into the knowledge and experience of distantly located colleagues, federal laboratories, private sector consultants, and other resources. *TECnet* users include personnel located at the various Manufacturing Extension Partnership sites, manufacturers, consultants, and service providers at universities, national laboratories, and other organizations. Technical databases offer information on topics such as best manufacturing practices, materials and chemicals, waste recycling, quality standards, and trade opportunities. As appropriate, *TECnet* personnel will direct requests for technical assistance to manufacturing-related user groups and electronic bulletin boards that are also accessible over the Internet.

How Do I Use It?

Connect to *TECnet* using any World Wide Web software such as Netscape or Mosaic, or through a service such as Prodigy, Compuserve, or America Online. One may access its World Wide Web site through the following URL: *http://www.technet.org*. Once at the TECnet Home Page, one must have subscriber access to utilize *TECnet's* features.

Cost

Contact the *TECnet* office for current individual and group rates.

Strengths and Weaknesses for Users

TECnet includes the following useful features:

- point-and-click interface for simple Internet navigation;
- electronic mail;
- information from local and international sources;
- ability to find the best information and services relevant to specific fields;
- access to industry experts;
- up-to-date information about legislation and policy developments; and
- opportunities to network and learn with colleagues worldwide.

User Base

Not available.

User Support

	N/A	Available	Comments
Consultants	x		
Documentation		x	
Training Classes	x		
Telephone Support		x	

Vendor Contact

TECnet
Tufts University
4 Colby Street, Room 153
Medford, MA 02155
VOICE (617) 627-3818
FAX (617) 623-1427
E-MAIL support@tecnet.org
URL http://www.tecnet.org

USING NEW TECHNOLOGIES: A TECHNOLOGY TRANSFER GUIDEBOOK (VERSION 2.0)

DESCRIPTION

Created by the Software Productivity Consortium, this guidebook is primarily concerned with adopting and implementing technologies. Although this publication offers an integrated approach to technology transfer based on research and experience across multiple states, it draws heavily upon the Consortium's Evolutionary Spiral Process (ESP) and is derived from a software engineering context. ESP offers guiding principles and practices in three areas: change management, which aids efforts to gain transfer support; risk management, which helps identify and avert risks to transfer; and project management, which offers increased management visibility, support, and ultimately, control of the transfer. The guidebook is particularly oriented toward professional managers or engineers responsible for implementing new technology in their organizations. Although originally designed to promote productivity improvement at software development organizations, the guidebook features many examples applicable to technology transfer at any organization.

HOW DO I USE IT?

Using New Technologies: A Technology Transfer Guidebook is organized into eight sections: motivating technology transfer; understanding the technology transfer process; understanding the context of one's situation; analyzing risks and selecting strategy; planning technology implementation; technology implementation; transfer plan review and updating; and improving one's technology transfer process. The guidebook also offers three checklists for applying the technology transfer process.

COST

Using New Technologies: A Technology Transfer Guidebook is available for $20.

STRENGTHS AND WEAKNESSES FOR USERS

This is a well-organized, pragmatic approach for planning and implementing technology transfer. While some technology transfer material can be faulted for focusing solely on the technological factors of transfer, this guidebook also examines the human issues of transfer such as the impact upon organizational culture and typical human responses to perceived change. The guide is better suited to more experienced technology transfer professionals, however, than to novices. One potential shortcoming is its primary focus on software engineering, the field from which most of the examples are drawn.

USER BASE

The second version of the guidebook has been available since December 1993 and has been well-received throughout the technology transfer community. It was produced by the Software Productivity Consortium Services Corporation under contract to the Virginia Center of Excellence for Software Reuse and Technology Transfer.

USER SUPPORT

	N/A	Available	Comments
Consultants	x		
Documentation	x		
Training Classes	x		
Telephone Support	x		

VENDOR CONTACT

SPC
2214 Rock Hill Road
Herndon, VA 22070
VOICE   (703) 742-7211
E-MAIL   eward@software.org

WRIGHT LABORATORY MANUFACTURING TECHNOLOGY DIRECTORATE PROJECT BOOK 1995

DESCRIPTION

The *Wright Laboratory Manufacturing Technology Directorate Project Book 1995* is a "living" document with the specific purpose of promoting the transfer of technology developed under previous programs. It is a warehouse of information with more than 120 projects described in detail, with most having technical reports available upon request. This reservoir of information covers a spectrum of technologies including computer integration, metals, composites, and electronics.

HOW DO I USE IT?

The *Project Book* is arranged according to topic category. Users should look up projects in the area that interests them. A written request on company letterhead is needed to process any document requested. Such a letter should include: the title of document, contract or technical report number; reason for document request; and typed name, title, mailing address, and signature.

COST

The *Project Book* is free. Requested technical reports are also free of charge.

STRENGTHS AND WEAKNESSES FOR USERS

The *Project Book* offers a comprehensive source of information that can be used by a variety of enterprises to obtain reports on current state-of-the-art technology. Users will find that each summary contains an explanation of the need for the project, the approach taken to accomplish the effort, the benefits expected to be realized, the current status, the name of the project engineer, and the performing contractor.

The Wright Laboratory Manufacturing Technology Directorate is tasked to ensure America's defense aerospace industrial base is fully capable and responsive in supporting Air Force needs in the development, production, and support of planned and existing weapon systems and components. Program successes frequently find broad application throughout defense and nondefense manufacturing sectors. The program is committed to enhancing domestic productivity, increasing quality, and reducing weapon systems acquisition and life-cycle costs.

USER BASE

The Technology Transfer Center's library has almost 4,000 documents available, and disseminates about 100 documents a month. Another technology transfer document, the *Program Status Report*, is distributed to 4,000 customers. People requesting the *Project Book* will placed on the *Program Status Report* mailing list.

USER SUPPORT

	N/A	Available	Comments
Consultants	x		Project engineers are available to answer questions about projects.
Documentation		x	
Training Classes	x		
Telephone Support		x	

VENDOR CONTACT

WL/MTX
Bldg. 653
Technology Transfer Center
2977 P St., Suite 6
Wright-Patterson AFB, OH 45433-7739
VOICE   (513) 256-0194
FAX   (513) 256-1422